Coping

Sexism

Rhoda McFarland

ROSEN PUBLISHING GROUP, INC./NEW YORK

Published in 1990 by The Rosen Publishing Group, Inc.
29 East 21st Street, New York, NY 10010

First Edition

Manufactured in the United States of America

Library of Congress Cataloging-in-Publication Data

McFarland, Rhoda
    Coping with Sexism/ Rhoda McFarland
        p.   cm.
    Includes bibliographical references.
    Summary: Examines sex-oriented discrimination at work, in the
media, at school, and at play, and provides tips on how to deal with it.
    ISBN 0-8239-1175-6
    1. Sex discrimination against women—United States—Juvenile
literature.   2. Sexism—United States—Juvenile literature. [1. Sex
discrimination against women.   2. Sexism.]
    HQ1426.M394   1990
    305.3′0973—dc20   90-30665
                                                            CIP
                                                            AC

ABOUT THE AUTHOR ⋄

Rhoda McFarland is a Certified Alcohol/Drug Counselor. She is a former teacher with experience teaching kindergarten through community college. She has been a faculty member of the Breining Institute for training counselors in alcoholism and other dependencies.

Ms. McFarland has worked with troubled young people and their parents in schools and in the community. She is responsible for establishing the parent self-help group using *toughlove* philosophy in Sacramento, California. She wrote and implemented the first educational program in the central California area for students making the transition from drug/alcohol treatment programs back into the regular school system.

Currently a Peace Corps Volunteer in Belize, Central America, Ms. McFarland continues to share her knowledge and expertise in the field of chemical dependency. She works with a community drug education/prevention agency. She also teaches a drug education class at the community college level and assists the Belize Curriculum Development Department in the training teachers decision-making skills, and coping with peer pressure.

A longtime choir director and musician, Ms. McFarland played bass clarinet in the Sacramento Valley Symphonic Band, a community organization of nonprofessional musicians. Since there is no community band in Belize, she expresses her musical talents as a member of the Belize Choral Society. Other hobbies include reading, travel, sewing, and snorkeling on Belize's world renowned barrier reef.

Contents

CHAPTER ◇ 1

Sexism

The sound of the door slamming gave Chris great satisfaction. She knew her mother wouldn't be happy about it, but that was just too bad. She was mad, and she didn't care who knew it. That Mr. Crawford was nothing but a male chauvinist pig. How dare he treat her that way!

One look at Chris's face and Georgia Hollis knew that something was very wrong with her daughter. This was not the girl who had left the house an hour and a half earlier. When Georgia asked what was going on, it took several minutes of hearing Mr. Crawford called a sexist bigot, male chauvinist pig, degrader of women, stupid jerk, and male supremacist before she got the story.

Chris had been walking by Mr. Crawford's print shop when she noticed a help wanted sign. Mr. Crawford had been standing in the doorway as Chris read the sign. He had said good morning, and she had returned the greeting and asked what kind of job opening he had. He had smiled and said, "Well, I'll tell you, honey, I sure wish it was something I could hire you to do. I'd like to have a cute little thing like you around." Chris had been so astounded that she was speechless, and Mr. Crawford had gone inside before she had recovered. Now she had plenty to say. She knew girls in her school who would have been flattered to be called a "cute little thing," but Chris felt it was degrading. She also resented being called "honey" as though she were a nonperson lumped in with all the other "sweet" female nonpersons. The implication that she was incompetent or incapable of doing a job because she was a female was the most infuriating of all.

As her mother listened without interrupting, Chris realized that this was old stuff to her. In fact, it was Georgia who had made her aware of the patronizing, insulting way some men treated women. Chris paused, then said, "Mom, what makes people like that?"

"There's no simple answer to that, Chris. The roots of that kind of patronizing put-down go way back. Since primitive times women have been looked on from a sexual point of view as serving a functional purpose and bearing children. The fact that all women share the same biology, or physiology, has caused them to be classified under one general concept. It boils down to the attitude that women are here for the sexual pleasure of men. If your looks please them, you should be grateful when they let you know it. Crass comments like Mr. Crawford's are considered compliments. They're so much a part of the culture that some women not only encourage them but actively seek them."

"It's not just older men like Mr. Crawford who talk that way," Chris said. "Boys in school stand in the halls and make comments. One of the boys in my math class told me that the guys have a rating system. He wouldn't tell me what it was, and he turned red. I figured it must be pretty gross. You know, they have to be so tough and macho; real men. They're really hung up on being manly."

"That comes from sex-role stereotyping," Georgia explained, "and that starts when a person is born; probably before. I remember that people gave me yellow baby things before you were born and pink things after. Nobody gave me anything blue because you were a girl, and blue is for boys. Your grandmother was appalled when we bought you that dump truck you wanted when you were three. Girls aren't supposed to play with dump trucks, according to her."

"That was one of my favorite things. I didn't know then that trucks were supposed to be for boys."

"How about now?" Georgia asked.

"Well, uh..."

They both laughed, and Georgia said, "Pretty sexist thinking if you ask me."

As they talked, Chris could see that sexism involved a lot more than she had ever considered. She looked up the definition of sexism in *Webster's Ninth New Collegiate Dictionary* and read, "1. prejudice or discrimination based on sex; *esp*: discrimination against women 2. behavior, conditions, or attitudes that foster stereotypes of social roles based on sex." The second part of the definition opened up a discussion with her mother about the many ways that people reinforce sex-role stereotyping.

Chris thought of how often in elementary school she had done something or wanted to do something and some adult had said, "Nice little girls don't do that." She had climbed a tree one time, and a neighbor had told her to come right down because girls don't climb trees. When she had told her parents about it, her father had asked, "Do you climb trees?" At Chris's nod, he said, "Well, then, girls do climb trees." Reminding her mother of that incident, Chris remembered how relieved she had been that it was okay for girls to climb trees.

Chris brought up the fact that in school the teachers

expected boys and girls to follow sex-role stereotypes. When the chemistry teacher asked who was interested in being a lab assistant, several girls had raised their hands along with four boys. The teacher had told the girls to put down their hands because the job required moving boxes of supplies. Chris felt that she was capable of being a good lab assistant, and moving boxes was no big deal. Eliminating girls because "girls are weak and boys are strong" was definitely stereotypic thinking.

Classes are considered masculine or feminine. In Chris's school it was hard to get boys to join the choir because singing wasn't "macho." There was a special auto mechanics class for girls.

Georgia reminded Chris of the time she had brought her first-grade reader home and asked why the mother in the stories was always in the house. Chris had said they never had Moms doing things that Moms do. "The Moms never play catch with the kids the way you do, and they never take the dogs for a walk or paint the house like you and Daddy did on Saturday." That called for further discussion on how women are portrayed in children's books. Soon they were talking about cartoons on TV.

"Look at the "Smurf" cartoons," Chris remarked. There's only one adult-type female and one little girl. All the rest are males, and Papa Smurf runs everything. That's pretty sexist, Mom. I never thought about it before, but there aren't any females in "Bugs Bunny" cartoons, at least not on a regular basis. In "Fat Albert" they are all males, and Sylvester and Tweetie are males. The guys have all the fun. Then the commercials push Barbie dolls for girls."

"Commercials are what get to me," Georgia said. "Men portray the macho image, and women are fluff and sex appeal in most of them. Look at who advertises what. Most of the narrations for commercials are done by men.

Women sell stockings, perfume, feminine hygiene products, some cleaning products, and add the sex to beer and wine ads.

Then Georgia brought up the stereotyping in soap operas. "Oh, Mom, it's so dramatic, and everybody has such horrible problems, and the love affairs are so romantic and stormy..."

"And all the women have to have a man or their lives aren't worth living, and they cry and the big, strong man says he'll take care of them, and the nasty, hateful, snake woman is always trying to break up the lovers, and on and on." By this time Chris and Georgia were laughing.

They talked on about how the media reinforce sex stereotypes, and then Chris mentioned work. She had heard her parents discuss sex discrimination in the workplace for years. The Hollises owned a construction company. Richard handled the job sites. He hired and ran the crews and did everything necessary to see that the job was done right and things ran smoothly. Georgia handled the business end. She bid all the jobs, dealt with the subcontractors, ordered materials, and made sure that everything was at the job site when it was needed. She took care of the finances. She had help in the office with the paperwork and the payroll, but Georgia hassled with individuals or companies that were late paying their bills and explained to creditors that they'd get their money as soon as Hollis Construction got the money owed them. Often men hadn't wanted to talk to Georgia because she was a woman. They wanted the "head man." Georgia had learned to be very assertive. Her standard line was, "The head man here is a woman."

Breaking into a "man's world" had given Georgia some special insights into sex discrimination. She was also aware of the problems of women in traditionally female positions.

"You know, Chris, many jobs held by women are low-paying because women have always done those jobs and have been poorly paid for them. A major reason there aren't more male clerical workers is because men won't work for such low wages. In fact, single women who have to support themselves won't take such low-paying jobs. It's married women who work in most of those jobs. And that could lead us into another area that I really can't get into now. There's work to do around here. How about some help?"

Two days later Chris stopped by the office on the way home from school. "We're having a meeting at our house tonight. Shall I stop by the store and get some Cokes and chips and stuff? We don't have any at home."

"Fine with me," Georgia agreed. "What's going on?"

Chris explained that their English teacher had assigned a group research project on any subject of current importance. Since the discussion about sexism was still in Chris's mind, she had suggested that for a topic, and the group had agreed. "The meeting tonight is to pool resources and plan our presentation," Chris concluded.

As the meeting broke up that evening, each member of the group had a specific topic on which to gather information and report back the following week. The three boys insisted that the presentation be nonsexist and present a balanced picture. "How can it be balanced when the whole world is so male-dominated?" protested Pam Chee.

"You may think so, but my mother nags me at home, female teachers nag me at school, my girlfriend nags me away from school, and my boss at the Hamburger Hut is a woman. My world is a long way from being male-dominated!" Paul Rodriguez complained.

"Okay, okay. We get the point. Maybe we're all in for

some surprises," said Colleen Madigan. "I'm anxious to see what you guys come up with."

"Guys, you called us guys. We're men, and don't you forget it," chided Alex Richards, with a "Hear, hear" from Stan Youngman.

"Out, out, all of you," laughed Chris, "before it comes to blows. We meet here after school next Wednesday."

WHAT IS SEXISM?

Sexism is a mind-set. Behavior is based on beliefs and values and attitudes, and all of those things are a result of the way you think, the set of your mind. When Chris looked up the meaning of sexism, she found two definitions; one narrow and specific, the other much broader. "Discrimination based on sex; especially discrimination against women," is very specific. Outright discrimination against women is relatively easy to see, such as Chris's teacher who told the girls to put down their hands or a man's refusing to talk to Georgia and demanding the head man. Much more sexism is hidden or camouflaged and comes under the second definition: "behavior, conditions, or attitudes that foster stereotypes of social roles based on sex."

Indirect sex-role stereotyping is so much a part of the culture that people do it without realizing it. It's sad that children can be so limited by sexist stereotyping. Chris wouldn't have enjoyed the fun of a dump truck or the thrill of climbing trees if her parents had the typical attitude about the kinds of toys and activities that are suitable for a girl.

Cartoons and storybooks don't say, "Boys have more fun than girls," but they always show boys having the exciting adventures. Many girls have sat on the sidelines and wished they were boys so they could do the things that boys do. Very few boys have watched girls enviously, wishing they could be girls so they could do what girls do.

The "boys are better" myth is very much a part of the society. When children are small and girls are physically more mature than boys, it's not unusual for a father to say, "You're not going to let that girl beat you, are you? You'll have to try harder." It's always, "My dad can beat your dad." not "My mom can beat your mom." Who cares if your mom can beat mine? It's dads who count.

The women's movement from the beginning has been concerned with the problem of the dehumanizing of women, the treating of women as objects. Seeing women as sex objects is still very much a part of the stereotype that young men learn. Talking of conquests in the locker room is always in order. Comments about various parts of a woman's anatomy still bring laughs and leers. The boys at Chris's school enjoyed that pastime. That it is degrading and sexist was of no concern to them. The boy who told Chris about it was embarrassed because he knew it to be insulting; but if the young men were confronted, they would just claim to be having a little fun, not hurting anybody.

Television commercials and magazine ads use sexism to sell everything but the attitude that women are capable, competent human beings. Women portrayed as successful career women discard that image when the workday is over and revert to being sexy and seductive for some man by using the right perfume, toothpaste, or gourmet frozen dinner.

Stereotypes go deep, and sexism and discrimination against women are not limited to men. Women unthinkingly or insensitively pass on the stereotypes. Sexism is so much a part of life that women must be taught about it as much as men. Women have accepted their role for so long that they are often unaware of discrimination. Men have to live up to their stereotypes, and sexism is a big part of the male stereotype. "What makes people like that?" Chris asked. The seeds were planted long ago, and the roots go deep.

THE ROOTS OF SEXISM

The answer to Chris's question begins long ago. Throughout history men have dominated society. Women have not shared in political power. In Greece, 2,500 years ago, women were classified with slaves as far as rights were concerned. Aristotle and other philosophers took male superiority for granted. Roman law placed women under their husbands' rule, as did English law. Colonial laws followed English law, so women had no rights in early America.

Men's work has always been valued more than women's. This was true in primitive societies where women were the gatherers and men the hunters. Women provided most of the food for the tribe. In comparison to the total food supply, the meat provided by the hunters was very little, yet there were celebrations when the hunters returned. What they brought was valued above what the women supplied.

In our society today, Georgia could have told Chris that it's not unusual for a woman to give up a good job when her husband is transferred. His job is valued above hers. A prime example of this type of sacrifice was the resignation of Elizabeth Dole as Secretary of Transportation so that she could devote herself to her husband's campaign to become the Republican candidate for President in 1988. According to the New York *Times*, she "expressed reluctance to leave her post" but "she bowed to intense pressures by her husband's campaign aides who insisted that her full-time participation in the Presidential drive was crucial."

Georgia was correct when she said that biology forced women to be mothers and society imposed that as their primary, and often only, function. From earliest times women have been associated with home and children because, out of necessity, they gave birth to children and cared for them. As a result, it became "natural"—like nature—for women to be considered only in their role of mother. The attitude that grew out of that is pretty well summed up in this passage from the Holy Koran of Islam: "Creator of the heavens and the earth, He has given you wives from among yourselves to multiply you, and cattle male and female. Nothing can be compared with Him."

Islam isn't the only religion that promotes the subordination of women. In the Hindu Code of Manu, V, is found, "In childhood a woman must be subject to her father; in youth, to her husband; when her husband is dead, to her sons. A woman must never be free from subjugation." The Confucian Marriage Manual has this advice for women: "The five worst infirmities that afflict the females are indocility, discontent, slander, jealousy, and silliness... Such is the stupidity of woman's character, that it is incumbent upon her, in every particular, to distrust herself and to obey her husband."

Most religions in the United States derive from the Judeo-Christian tradition, which has its share of sexism. The Apostle Paul said, "Let the women learn in silence with all subjection...suffer not a woman to usurp authority over men, but to be in silence." A man who believes that is the way the world should be run would find it difficult to have a woman supervisor. Wouldn't it be hard to take a female coworker who was assertive and not afraid to show her intelligence? Georgia dealt with that issue every day. Perhaps being Jewish had something to do with St. Paul's attitude, since he was brought up on this Daily Orthodox Jewish Prayer: "I thank thee, O Lord, that thou hast not created me a woman."

With the attitude that men are better than women, that men's work is more important than women's, it was natural that the belief that men are smarter than women would be common. For centuries, schools were for boys only, and wealthy boys at that. If girls went to school, it was to learn manners, how to dress, how to speak politely; in short, how to be a lady. Women were considered to be intellectually inferior and to have no need for education. An old Chinese proverb states: "The glory of a man is knowledge, but the glory of a woman is to renounce knowledge." Samuel Johnson dealt with women's intellect in this way: "A man in general is better pleased when he has a good dinner than when his wife talks Greek."

You could say that all of those things were written at a time when women weren't considered to be people, when the world was ignorant and unenlightened. However, in this "englightened age" those beliefs are still very much alive and active. They are not so openly expressed, but anyone who says, "The way to a man's heart is through his stomach," subscribes to Samuel Johnson's view of women.

Our government is based on the Constitution, which states that all men are created equal. Of course, we're assured that "men" really meant mankind, men and women. They did really mean "men" though, Georgia was certain. When the Constitution was written women had no political power. Economically they were dependent on fathers and husbands. Women brought property to marriage, but their husbands managed all property and financial affairs.

When this free, democratic society was established, women and slaves were not allowed to vote. The slaves were freed in 1861, and shortly afterward the Fourteenth Amendment said that no one could be kept from voting because of race, color, or creed, thereby giving male blacks the right to vote. Georgia wondered if Chris's history teachers taught about women's struggle to gain the vote.

When women sought to be included under the Fourteenth Amendment, they failed. Susan B. Anthony led that fight. A black woman, Sojourner Truth, also worked hard for the cause. The first meeting of women for equal rights was held in Seneca, New York, in the home of Elizabeth Cady Stanton. Mrs. Stanton and Lucretia Mott called a conference at which women demanded equal job and educational opportunities and abolishment of laws that discriminated against them because of sex. All of their attempts to influence legislation failed, so in 1869 Mrs. Stanton founded the National Women's Suffrage Association. In the same year Lucy Stone founded a less militant group called the American Woman Suffrage Association. In 1890 the two groups merged into the National American Woman Suffrage Association and worked for almost thirty years to gain the vote for women.

Finally, in 1920 the Nineteenth Amendment passed, giving women the right to vote. Unfortunately, however, gaining the vote still didn't insure women equal rights. Women fought for years to get the Equal Rights Amendment ratified, but it failed to gain approval of the necessary two thirds of state legislatures. Georgia knew the disappointment of that defeat. Now, 120 years after the first women's meeting for equal rights, American women are still fighting for those same rights.

CHAPTER 2

What's the
Difference?

"Hi, Gina, are you working on the project?"
Gina Augustino looked up to see Ellen
Peterson standing by the table where she
sat outside the public library.

"Oh, hi, Ellen. Yeah, I'm trying to get this stuff organized. It's more interesting than I thought it would be, but it's going to take some work to sort it out and put it together. I hate to spend my Saturday at the library, but at least I can sit outside and still have the library handy. Have you started working on yours?"

Ellen sat down and admitted that she had come to the library to get started. She had kept putting off work on her part of the project, but she couldn't any longer because the next meeting was set for Wednesday.

Ellen asked if Gina knew what each member of the group was doing. "Eight of us are working on it," Gina said, "and I didn't write down who's doing what. I'm supposed to find out if we're born with feminine or masculine traits or if we learn to be feminine or masculine. You know, what's the difference between boys and girls, that sort of thing."

"Well, aren't the differences pretty obvious?"

"Physical differences, yes, but some other things aren't so obvious. At least, how some things got the way they are isn't that easy to see." Gina said that most physical differences had to do with size and strength and vigor. There are 105 males born for every 100 females, but about 33 percent more baby boys die than baby girls. Childhood illnesses kill more boys than girls. Baby girls may be stronger than boys because they're about six weeks more mature when they're born. A newborn girl is physiologically equal to a six-week-old boy.

"Most girls are ahead of boys by about eighteen months in bone development, in getting permanent teeth, in reaching puberty, and in overall physical maturity," Gina said.

"I'll bet the boys won't be happy to hear about that," Ellen remarked. "They think they're so rough and tough."

Gina went on to say that in a way boys *are* rough and tough. At least they have larger bones, greater muscle mass, and physical strength as they grow up. They develop better motor skills such as running, jumping, and throwing. Although until about thirteen or fourteen girls and boys are the same in height and weight, by twenty most males are five to six inches taller than most females. Boys continue to improve in physical performance longer than girls, and by about age twenty the average male can match the best female in athletic performance—speed, strength, and skill.

"You'd better not let Colleen hear that, or you'll have a fight on your hands," Ellen cautioned.

"She won't need to get too excited. Just because those

are the average statistics, it doesn't mean that people can't go beyond them. I read an article in *Sports Illustrated* about a jockey named Julie Krone. She's 4 foot 10½ and weighs something like 104 pounds. She decided she was going to be a top jockey, and she is. Nobody thought women had the strength to control a half ton of horseflesh down the stretch of a demanding race. No one thought women could withstand the rough tactics that it takes to win races. Well, Julie Krone proved that women can ride with the best of men and hold their own in the macho world of thoroughbred horse racing.

"Female athletes have been gradually closing the gap between men's and women's records in Olympic running events. Female swimmers today swim faster than the Olympic records of men in the past. Average sex differences are just that: average. Colleen's a great athlete, and she doesn't have to let anything stop her."

"Don't you think there are some things that girls do and some that boys do?" Ellen wanted to know.

"Like what?" Gina asked.

"Well, you know, girls are more into clothes and shopping and..."

"Oh, you mean like girls play with dolls and boys play with trucks; and boys are more aggressive and girls are more the peacemaker; stuff like that," Gina broke in.

"Yeah. That's what I mean."

Leaning over the table toward Ellen, Gina began to tell her what she had found in her research. Everything she had found, Gina said, referred to the work of Eleanor Maccoby and Carol Jacklin, two psychologists from Stanford University. They had studied hundreds of behaviors that were supposed to be the result of sex differences and could find only four actual differences between the sexes: (1) Males are more aggressive than females; (2) girls have greater verbal ability than boys; (3) boys have superior visual-spatial ability; and (4) boys are superior in mathematical/analytical ability.

"I pretty much agree that boys are more aggressive than girls," Ellen said, "but I know some girls who are pretty aggressive. I'm not so sure about the superiority in mathematical ability. The two best math students in school are Jane Hill and Kathy Westin. The boys are always complaining about them."

"That's a good point, Ellen, because it brings out another thing that was found out. There's much more difference within each sex than there is between the sexes. For example, among children playing the amount of activity and behavior rated aggressive was much greater between the most passive girl and the most aggressive girl than it was between the average girl and the average boy."

"But boys and girls do act different," Ellen said. "Even little kids do. I take care of my neighbor's little boy. When his friends come over to play, they run around outside and crash trucks and make all kinds of noise. When I baby-sit girls and their friends come over, they usually want to play dolls or play dress-up or something like that. If I tell them they have to play outside, they collect all the doll stuff and sit in the yard and play. They do ride bikes and roller skate, but they mostly play girl things."

"That's true," Gina agreed, "but how much of that is influenced by what they're given to play with or what's advertised on TV or what they see boys and girls doing? Remember in social science when we had that big discussion about nature or environment? It's hard to know if we do something because it's biological or natural for us when so much is influenced by where we live and the people around us."

Looking puzzled and thoughtful, Gina told Ellen that

she was trying to sort out the difference between gender and sex role. "You know, we all know whether we're a boy or girl by the time we're one and a half to three years old. And that's really important. Once we know what gender we are, we have to keep proving it to ourselves. You know, I'm a girl so I watch what other girls do, and then I act like them. At least that's what Dr. Joseph Pleck, an expert on sex roles, says."

"So gender identity is knowing that I'm a girl," Ellen said. "What is sex role then?"

"As I understand it, sex role is the behavior we learn," Gina explained. "It's what society considers the right kind of behavior for girls or boys. It's things like females are supposed to be soft and sweet, weak, passive, take care of house and children, support their men. Men are supposed to be strong, tough, fearless, aggressive, earn the money for the family, all that macho stuff.

"Dr. Pleck says that you go through stages so that you finally realize that you don't have to stick to sex roles, that you can just be a human being and enjoy activities, feelings, behavior, whatever, without worrying about whether it's okay for females or males. For instance, Colleen plays on the soccer team because she's every bit as good as the boys."

"Lots of people think it's wrong for Colleen to be on the team," Ellen said.

"That's their sexist thinking. It's limiting and keeps people from becoming the most they can be," Gina told her. "What I'm working on now is finding out how parents and other adults influence sex-role development in young children. I want to know how we can keep from passing on the stereotypes."

The girls talked a few minutes longer, and then Ellen went into the library to get material for her part of the project. Gina got back to her reading. About an hour later Ellen came out with several books and stopped to check on Gina's progress. Since Gina was about finished, she asked Ellen to wait while she returned some books, and then the girls walked together. As they walked they continued talking about sex-role stereotyping.

"I never thought about it before," Ellen said slowly, "but I do it with babies. If I know it's a girl, I say, 'Isn't she sweet,' or something like that. If it's a boy, I always comment on how big he is or what a lady-killer he's going to be. That's really sexist, isn't it?"

Gina told Ellen that people handle boy babies differently from girls. Fathers particularly are rougher with boys than they are with girls. More girls than boys are spoken to in high-pitched voices, and the talk is usually gentler. Boys are more likely to hear things such as, "What's this rascal been up to today!" or "Come here, you little devil, and say hello to Daddy."

In one study Gina read about, six-month-old girls were held and cuddled and spoken to more often than boys the same age. In another study of young children it was found that parents encouraged boys to be more active and disapproved if they were more quiet and passive. Girls were encouraged to be passive and quiet. Parents don't want their boys to be "sissies." They look on the aggressive behavior of sons and say, "Boys will be boys."

Expectations for girls and boys are different. When children don't live up to the expectations, they hear things like, "Big boys don't cry," and "Be a nice girl and sit down and play with your toys."

As Gina and Ellen walked, they talked about the effect that sex-role stereotypes had on them. Gina was resentful because her brothers never had to do the dishes or change the beds or do any other housework. They washed the car and cut the grass and did all the "masculine" things. She confided that she would rather mow the lawn than clean the bathroom any day.

Being hassled by the boys in driver education class bothered Ellen. She was tired of comments about women drivers. If a boy made a mistake, no one said anything. If she made a mistake, they made a big deal about it. "Women have been driving for years and years, and their accident rate is lower than men's; yet the old stereotype is still thrown up to us," Ellen complained.

Old stereotypes don't go away easily, both girls agreed. Little girls still get dolls, tea sets, and stoves to prepare them for being mothers and housekeepers. They don't get briefcases or toolboxes to prepare them for future jobs. Ellen told Gina about a friend of hers whose parents were divorced. "For Mother's Day last year her mother asked for a three-quarter-inch reversible drill. She and her sister couldn't believe it at first, but her mother said that when they moved she would need it to take the waterbeds apart and put them together again and to put up the curtain and drapery rods. I thought it was weird when Connie told me about it, but now I realize that was because it didn't fit the sex-role stereotype for a mother."

"I'm in the choir," Gina said, "and it's really hard for us to get boys to join because they say it's only for wimps. It was only a few years ago that girls were first allowed to take mechanical drawing; it was always for boys only. Mechanical drawing doesn't prepare you for motherhood, I guess."

The girls began to talk about "feminine" and "masculine" things, and they realized that it's much more acceptable for girls to be interested in things that are considered masculine than for boys to be interested in things that are considered feminine. Girls can play softball or a trombone or take karate and be accepted. Boys who want to take ballet or learn to sew are labeled "gay" or "fairy."

After Ellen turned onto her street, Gina continued to walk slowly and think about the pressures that sex roles put on people. It seemed to her that boys had a really rough time if they didn't live up to the stereotypes. She thought of the boys she had dismissed because they were small or looked "weak and wimpy." She wondered how they felt about not being rough and tough. She knew that some of them had been teased and bullied by bigger boys when they were in grade school.

Gina remembered how much she had wanted to go fishing with her brothers and father, but her father said it was just for boys. She used to wish she were a boy.

As she turned up the walk to the house, Gina thought about the opportunities lost to both boys and girls because of sexism. "Boys and girls aren't the same, and nobody should try to make them the same," Gina thought, "but everyone deserves to make choices without having half the choices taken away before they start."

DIFFERENCES BETWEEN THE SEXES

Biological and Physical Differences. When Gina mentioned differences between boys and girls, Ellen immediately thought of the obvious biological differences. Children are born either male or female. If they're female, they have two X chromosomes, and after twelve weeks the XX chromosomes send a message to the gonads of the embryo to start developing ovaries to produce the hormones for female sexual characteristics. If the baby is a male, it has an X chromosome from its mother and a Y chromosome from its father. After just six weeks, the XY chromosomes send a message to the gonads to begin developing testes to produce the hormones for male sexual characteristics.

Normal males are capable of impregnating females, and normal females are capable of becoming pregnant and breast-feeding children. At about the age of fifty women go through biological changes and can no longer bear children. The reproductive capabilities of men usually last longer. Some men in their seventies have fathered children.

As Gina said, males on the average are bigger and stronger than females. However, if you were to judge by resistance to illness, genetic defects, and rate of maturity, males would be the "weaker" sex.

At one time it was very important for men to be bigger and stronger because survival depended on their strength. With technology in the twentieth century, talent has become much more important than muscle.

The boundaries of human strength and endurance in sports keep changing as new methods of training are developed. Women are achieving goals that were inconceivable in the past. In the U.S. Olympic Track and Field Trials in July, 1988, Florence Griffith Joyner ran 100 meters in 10.49 seconds. The crowd was shocked into silence. She not only shattered the women's record of 10.76, but her time would have won every men's Olympic record up until 1960.

Behavioral Differences.   Many studies have been done to find out what behaviors are definitely linked to sex. Gina told Ellen about Maccoby and Jacklin's study, which is recognized for its thoroughness. Other researchers have accepted their findings of four differences between the sexes: females have superior verbal skills; males, superior mathematical and visual-spatial abilities; males are more aggressive.

Maccoby and Jacklin found that males and females have equal IQs. To the age of ten, boys and girls score equally on math and verbal parts of IQ tests. After ten, girls begin to go ahead in verbal skills, outscoring boys in spelling, punctuation, vocabulary, reading comprehension, and understanding of logical relationships that are expressed in verbal terms. They also are superior in using language verbally and in creative writing.

By age thirteen boys begin to score much higher than girls in mathematics, and they keep the lead from then on. Some girls do excel in math, as Ellen pointed out. However, advanced math classes have an overwhelming majority of males. Some people believe that this superiority in mathematics may be related to their superior ability to see spatial relationships.

That boys are more aggressive than girls has been shown in study after study in a variety of cultures. Maccoby and Jacklin defined aggression as hostile actions such as hitting and threatening. Males are much more likely to threaten to hit someone and carry out the threat. Boys tend to be much more aggressive toward other boys than they are toward girls.

When boys are rowdy or aggressive, you often hear, "Boys will be boys," an attitude that tolerates more aggressive behavior from boys. Some parents punish boys more often and more firmly for aggressive behavior because they feel that boys need more control than girls. Although parents may not encourage boys to be aggressive, they may discourage them from behavior they feel to be "sissy." This may cause boys to be more aggressive just to prove that they aren't "sissy."

Whether encouraged, tolerated, or expected, Maccoby

and Jacklin say that aggression is learned, and biology prepares boys to learn it.

There are lots of boys who would rather read than play football, and girls who would rather play baseball with the boys than dolls with the girls. It is generally agreed, as Gina explained, that differences within each sex are much greater than average differences between the sexes. It's also true that many areas overlap—Colleen can play soccer as well as the boys; Kathy and Jane are better than the boys in math; the creative writing contest is won by a boy. It's important not to allow average differences between the sexes to limit your choices.

Gender Identity and Sex Roles. It is not unusual for people to confuse gender identity and sex role. Many adults are not aware that gender and sex role are two separate things.

Between eighteen months and three years children find out that they are either boy or girl. They hear themselves referred to as boy or girl. They see other children who are labeled boy or girl. Sometime before the age of five they become aware of the physical differences between boys and girls. It becomes very important to them to reassure themselves which they are. They look around to see how a girl or a boy acts, and they act like that. Boys learn very early that they must not act like girls. It isn't nearly as bad for a girl to do some of the things that boys do.

Young children take on sex roles they see around them to prove to themselves that they are definitely a boy or a girl. Even if parents make dolls available to boys and trucks to girls, share child care and housework, and are as non-sexist as possible in raising their children, the six-year-old is influenced by much more than parents. He or she learns the sex roles and rigidly observes them. Dr. Joseph Pleck calls this the *conformist stage* of sex-role development.

The process as described by Pleck has three stages. The first stage is the *amorphous stage*. Preschool children are not much concerned about sex roles. The preschool boy loves his stuffed doll and hugs it and carries it with him. When he becomes aware of his gender and notices how boys act, he moves into the second or *conformist stage*. The six-year-old gets rid of the doll because "Dolls are for girls."

The conformist phase lasts into adolescence. Boys tend to be much more concerned about their sex role than girls. It's during this time that girls hear, "She can't play," and "No girls allowed." Boys are constantly proving their masculinity. They can't allow any sign of weakness or softness that might be seen as a chink in their armor. They want to be with boys and do what boys do.

Girls also prefer same-sex friends. Birthday parties are usually all girls or all boys. However, because things masculine are valued, many girls want to do the things that boys do. It's okay for a girl to play baseball with the boys, but it's not okay for a boy to play jacks with the girls. Girls don't have to prove over and over that they're girls. It's not unusual for girls between six and twelve to wish they were boys.

A new intensity in the need to conform to sex role, similar to the discovery of gender identity, comes when the child become aware of genital sexuality. For most girls this is about age thirteen. For boys it's often a little later. To your parents' horror, you look to your peer group for your security and sense of belonging. You come home with all kinds of ideas about dress and behavior that may be very upsetting to your parents and other adults because of this new, intensified need to conform.

Once you've established a sense of security and belong-

ing, you can move to the third phase in sex-role development, the *transcendent phase*. To transcend is to go beyond
the limits. You realize that young women can change the
washer in the kitchen faucet, young men can dry the tears
of a three-year-old, you can wear an old shirt and jeans to
paint the house and a beautiful formal to the prom that
night, you can write a poem telling your father how much
you love him on his birthday and he'll be as proud of his
son as he was the day you scored the point that won the
basketball game. Yes, you can transcend traditional sex
roles and make decisions for yourself as to what is right for
you.

SEX ROLES AND YOU

As Gina learned more about sex-role stereotyping and
talked with Ellen about it, both girls became aware of how
sexism had affected them and how they had accepted and
applied the stereotypes to others. They could see how boys
and girls are treated differently from birth by parents and
other people too. Studies have shown that people don't
know what to say or how to treat babies when they don't
know their gender.

Gina wasn't given the opportunity to go fishing, cut the
grass, or do many other things that were considered outside her sex role as a girl. She is learning that she has
choices besides those given to her by her parents. As she
matures, she'll have more opportunity to make decisions
for herself. She'll be able to go fishing if she wants to, and if
she has a daughter one day, she can take her daughter
fishing if she wants. If Gina doesn't like to fish and would
rather go shopping, she can let her daughter go fishing
with her father or someone else.

The next time Ellen sees a baby boy, she can tell his

mother that he's a sweetie. She can comment on how strong the baby girl is. When she baby-sits she can see if the two-year-old girl likes to play the same chase and catch and wrestle game that the two-year-old boy down the street likes. Ellen can look at her expectations and see if she's expecting and encouraging different behavior from boys and girls.

All children and adolescents go through the conformist phase—or at least they reach it. The less sexist your environment, the more likely you are to pass through the conformist phase and get to transcendence. If you aren't aware of sexism in your environment, you may not know how your own attitudes have been and are being shaped. It's time to become aware of influences around you.

Parents, teachers, peers, relatives, churches, books, magazines, television, movies, leisure activities, and seemingly insignificant events and people work together to form your concept of sex roles. It's time to question what you see and hear. Women are interested in more than attracting men, no matter what the commercials imply. Men can be sensitive, feeling human beings without risking their manhood, and they needn't drink beer to prove they're real men either. You can be neat, clean, and helpful around the house regardless of your gender. Human beings get angry and need to show it; and human beings get hurt and need to cry. Feelings are not gender-specific, they're human-specific.

When sex-role lines are clearly drawn and you accept them and live them, you can be stuck in the conformist phase. Females, according to sex-role stereotypes, have been described as gentle, soft, delicate, weak, indecisive, passive, tender, sensitive, dependent, loving, submissive, warm, responsible, nurturing. Words connected to males are strong, powerful, decisive, independent, virile, courageous, unemotional, active, dominant, competent, aggressive, forceful, fearless, clever, vigorous.

People who develop only those characteristics traditionally associated with their gender are only half human beings. One side of their humanity is missing. Remove the gender association from the words above, and allow everyone to develop all of the attributes, and you will see whole human beings.

Many women want to erase the lines that limit women, but they don't consider the limits that are put on men by sexism. Some men can be very liberal-minded about women but still hold their stereotypes about men. What are your expectations of men? Are you letting them out of their box, too? Are you embarrassed or uncomfortable if a man cries, or do you see him as a feeling human being? Is your attitude toward softer, gentler men similar to Gina's, who labeled them "wimps," or are you able to say that not all human beings are alike or need to be?

When you see the lines between the sex roles blur and become less important; when doing the dishes doesn't threaten manhood and putting oil in the car isn't too complicated for a woman; when you can feel tender or forceful, loving or independent, fearful or decisive at appropriate times, you'll be moving into the transcendent phase. When you realize that males and females do the same things, you can begin to appreciate that they do them differently. When women first began pushing forward in business, they thought they had to be like men. They tried to copy the style of men even to dressing in a more severe, tailored fashion. Today women realize that they bring their own special talents to a job. Women use their competence, intelligence, and aggression in their own unique ways. By appreciating what men and women can each contribute to the situation, everyone is enriched.

Removing sex-role barriers means that everyone will have the opportunity to choose from the whole rather than being limited to half. When you transcend traditional sex roles, your map for the future is yours to create and the road yours to build.

CHAPTER 3

Sexism in Schools

Stan Youngman looked thoughtful as he leaned back in his chair and gazed out the window. Then he put his elbow on the table, his chin on his thumb, and his forefinger across his mouth and stared. "Jeez, man, what ya thinkin' about?"

Stan was jarred back to the present by Paul Rodriguez. "You looked like you were somewhere out in space."

"I guess I was, in a way," Stan said. "What're you doing at the library on a Saturday? Working on the project, too?" At Paul's nod, Stan said, "Ellen and Gina were leaving when I came. They were so busy talking they didn't even see me."

"You were so busy thinking, *you* didn't see *me*," remarked Paul. "What was that all about?"

"I was just thinking about how things were in elementary school. Pam and I are doing sexism in schools, and she found some stuff about how high school sexism affects girls, so she wanted to concentrate on that. I got stuck with sexism in elementary schools. I thought it was going to be boring or stupid, but what I've been reading has really made me think."

"Well, I don't expect mine to be boring, but I'm not sure what I'll find either," Paul confided. "I'm supposed to find out how males are affected by sexism. I got tired of hearing the girls complain about male chauvinists. I think female are just as bad sometimes. Now I have to find evidence to back that."

"I'm finding it in what I'm doing," Stan told him. "Or at least I'm finding that boys are as much affected as girls, especially in school. That's what I was thinking about when you got here. I was remembering what it was like in elementary school."

"I've got to get some work done right how, but how about going over to the Pit Stop for a shake or something after we get done here?" Paul suggested.

Later, over french fries and milk shakes, Paul asked Stan what he had been thinking about earlier. "I was trying to remember if what I was reading happened when we were in elementary school," Stan told him. "The more I thought about it, the more I could see that it did.

"First of all, it talked about how we learn sex roles and how those stereotypes are reinforced. You know, things like girls are supposed to be quiet and cooperative, and boys are aggressive and don't obey as well. Girls play house, and boys play with trucks and trains. Little kids see how men act and how women act and then try to act the same way. Girls can be interested in the same things as boys; they can play with Hot Wheels or play the same games as boys and it's okay. But if boys are interested in girl things or cry or act soft, they're called sissy and that's really bad. That's why boys don't want to do anything that might make people think they're a girl."

"Yeah," Paul agreed. "The stuff I've been reading says that boys learn really early that they're supposed to be strong and not be like girls. You know, we're supposed to 'take it like a man' no matter how much it hurts because 'big boys don't cry'."

"Teachers believe all the stereotypes, too," Stan continued, "so they expect boys to act rowdy and get into more trouble than girls. But, you see, they feel it's their job to tame us and make us act more civilized. Schools are run on females' terms, since the majority of elementary school teachers are women.

"Some people say that girls get the shaft because teachers pay more attention to boys. Maybe it's because boys get into more trouble so teachers are always after them. Even if it's negative attention, it's attention. Studies have shown that teachers talk to boys more about subject matter and listen to them more. Even when girls raise their hands, teachers call on boys more. Remember how the girls always hung around the teacher at recess?" At Paul's nod, Stan said, "Well, that's because girls want teachers' approval. One study said that even if you count that as teacher-student interaction, teachers still talked to boys more than they did to girls."

"All I know is that the girls were always the teacher's pets, and I couldn't move without getting in trouble," Paul grumbled.

"That's another thing the study said. Teachers don't discipline girls the way they do boys. They're harder on boys because boys can take it, according to the sex-role stereotype."

"So why do some people think girls have it so bad then?" Paul wanted to know.

"Girls are praised for being good, and they get the teacher's approval by being neat and doing their work and being smart. The more the girl conforms to the sex-role stereotype, the more approval she gets. That is supposed to stifle her and keep her from trying new things. Girls aren't as independent as boys. They don't risk new situations because they're praised for being dependent and compliant, according to the researchers. They say girls don't want to take chances of failing because they're afraid the teacher won't approve of them anymore."

"That isn't true about some girls I know, but most of them it would fit," Paul said. "Maybe that's why girls don't take advanced algebra and trig."

"That may be partly why," Stan agreed, "but one of the true sex differences is that boys do better in mathematics than girls. Maybe girls give up on math because it's harder than other subjects. They don't want to take the chance of failing and losing approval."

"This whole sexist thing is a lot more complicated than I thought." Paul pursed his lips while he thought and finally said, "What you're saying is that girls don't learn to push beyond what's easy for them. Since they get all their strokes from playing safe, they don't take the risk to try something that they don't know they can do well. I think they're afraid of math and chemistry and stuff like that."

"You could be right, but I'd have to check it out some more before I went that far," was Stan's cautious reply as the boys left the Pit Stop.

Later that evening Stan continued his research. He was particularly interested in finding out more about how teachers "feminize" boys. One author said that "feminize" meant weaken, make dependent, and squelch the spirit. However, most researchers seemed to agree that young boys rebel against having to be quiet and meek and manageable, and most succeed in keeping their independence. The rebellion brings more teacher disapproval, and thus more teacher attention in general. The more the boy refuses to obey the rules and be quiet, the more interaction he has with the teacher. As the boy keeps rebelling and doing things his own way, the more independent his approach to learning becomes.

Stan found that three things made researchers say that the feminine school atmosphere hurts boys. First was the effort to restrict their movement, not foster their independence. Stan had already looked at the other side of that. The second thing was boys' difficulty with reading. Stan could remember that there were always more girls in the best reading groups and more boys in the low groups. Boys got more comments such as "Pay attention!" "Sit still!" "Turn around and listen." The researchers said that boys didn't get to read as much either. Maybe negative comments don't hurt in the area of independence, but Stan could see that so much negativity could sure turn you off to reading. Thinking about it, he could see how you could get totally turned off to school if all you heard was what a jerk you are or how you're not trying.

Finally, even though they score the same on IQ and achievement tests, grade-school boys as a group get lower grades than girls. Stan could remember that girls were always considered the smartest ones in the class in elementary school. Somewhere along the line things changed—at least in some subjects. Stan read a little further and found what he was looking for. By age thirteen girls drop behind in math, science, and social studies. It's not until seventeen that girls fall back in reading and literature. Because they've gotten so much approval for not being aggressive or independent, and they haven't been encouraged to take risks, girls may not grow intellectually. Their ability may actually decrease.

When Stan read that as children grow older their opinion of boys goes up and their opinion of girls gets lower, he was skeptical. As he read, Stan began remembering experiences that proved the point to be true. In elementary school the stories that Stan remembered as favorites had boys as the main characters. The girls always liked those stories, too. In one article Stan read, an instructor of a writing class said that books should be written to attract boys because girls will read books about boys, but boys won't read books about girls.

In some ways Stan could see that it wasn't so much devaluing the female as putting emphasis and value on the male. He remembered that in his readers in elementary school boys got to do all the exciting things. The things that girls did weren't exciting at all. Who would want to be a girl? He hadn't realized that girls could lose self-esteem simply because they were girls, but that's what seemed to happen, according to several researchers. Girls are rewarded for being dependent and compliant. They don't want to take risks for fear of failure and disapproval. They see women in life and in books who bow to the authority of men and who are, apparently, inferior to men. These things diminish their self-worth.

"Wait a minute," thought Stan. "What's this bowing to male authority and inferior to men stuff?" That took him down another trail. Although the overwhelming majority of elementary school teachers are women, nationwide, less than 20 percent of the principals are female. In some states, only one in ten principals is female. Even though the classroom itself may be female-dominated, the ultimate authority is usually a male. Children see female teachers calling on the male principal to deal with misbehaving children (usually boys) that the teacher can't handle. The teacher is boss of the classroom, the principal is boss of the teacher, and the principal is a man. Men boss women is how the children interpret the situation.

Stan had to admit that he had bought into that stereo-type. It was true in business as well as school. He expected men to be in charge. Even though he knew women who were in authority, women like Mrs. Hollis and Mrs. Brown, the principal of Riverview High, he still expected men to be in positions of authority. Did that mean he thought women were inferior? That was a hard question, and Stan didn't want to look at it right then. He needed to think about all this stuff so he'd know what he wanted to report to the group on Wednesday. He realized that he had been influenced by sexism in elementary school. Paul had too. Stan wanted to hear the girls' reactions to all this and see if it checked out from their side. As he gathered up his materials he thought, "Wednesday is going to be an interesting day."

THE HIDDEN CURRICULUM

The courses offered at school are the curriculum. Besides the advertised courses, you also a get a course in sex-role stereotyping. The teachers of the course usually don't know they're teaching it, and students don't know they're taking it. That's why it's called the "hidden curriculum." Sex-role stereotyping is so automatic that you're unaware of it. Maccoby and Jacklin believe that teachers don't realize that they behave differently toward female and male students.

It is thought that because teachers consider girls different from boys, they expect different things from them and treat them differently. In preschool and primary grades, according to Maccoby and Jacklin, teachers value female and male pupils equally, but they describe their behavior differently. They described girls as being dependent and introverted and boys as aggressive and extroverted, even though observers saw no measurable differences in behavior. When preschool teachers were asked to rate boys and girls on activity, the teachers rated the boys as more active, but observers saw no differences between the sexes. The teachers were judging the children on the basis of sex stereotypes.

As Stan pointed out, studies show that teachers interact more with boys than with girls, both positively and negatively. They give more approval to boys' work and efforts than they do to girls' work. One theory of why this happens is that girls are considered neater, harder working, and better behaved, and it's assumed that they're doing their best. Since boys are stereotyped as careless and sloppy and not likely to do their best, teachers spend more time telling them they can do better if they try harder. When the boys do better, teachers then praise their efforts.

It was found that teachers give boys eight times more detailed instruction on how to solve problems themselves, but do the job or solve the problem for the girls. The message sent to boys is, "You're capable and can do it yourself," while the girls are clearly being told that they need help, that they are dependent.

Boys who misbehave receive considerably more attention than other students, but the attention is in the form of reprimands. On the other hand, girls who misbehave are given even less attention than other girls.

Much of the classroom misbehavior of boys is due to the confinement and forced inactivity. In the preschool years boys are allowed more freedom and encouraged to be more active than girls. When they go to school they're expected to stay in a small area, sit still, pay attention, and be quiet. To most boys, this is a new experience that they don't like, so they rebel against it. With the rebellion comes disapproval from the teacher. Like Paul, what they see is the girls being good and hanging around the teacher and being teacher's pets while they get jumped on for every little thing they do. This polarizes the sexes even more. Children feel the gulf between the sexes. Although Paul is a healthy teenager and likes girls today, there's still a part of him who is that little boy who hated teacher's pets.

CONSEQUENCES OF THE HIDDEN CURRICULUM

All children are affected by the hidden curriculum. There's great concern that the feminine atmosphere in school, especially in primary grades, is harmful to boys. Although preschool boys are usually in a "feminine" atmosphere at home—Father goes to work and Son stays home with Mother all day—the way boys are treated at home is very different from their treatment at school. At home they are encouraged to be independent. If Mother works they go to day care run by females; however, they're still allowed a great deal of freedom of movement. When they go to school, thirty children are in one classroom. Activity and independence are definitely not encouraged. The hidden curriculum is sit down, be still, and do what you're told. It's not surprising that many boys rebel.

It is the teacher's job to put down rebellion, and boys who don't behave are reprimanded. They receive lots of negative attention. But even with the increased attention, the little rebels don't always buy the idea of sit down and be quiet, and there's more interaction with the teacher. Some researchers found that, for some boys, this increased their independence. It becomes an attitude of "I'll do it my way."

A second, and more damaging, consequence of negative attention often occurs. The conflict at school can become so distressing that boys get turned off to school. When they're old enough to drop out, they do. Some drop out when they're still in the lower grades: Their bodies go to school, but their minds are anywhere but in the classroom.

Three times more boys than girls have reading problems. John McNeil did a study of 132 kindergarten children who were given identical, individual, programmed reading instruction. When they were tested, the boys made significantly higher scores than the girls. The children were then placed in a regular classroom with a female teacher. After four months they were tested, and the boys did not do as well as the girls. In talking with the children, McNeil found that more boys got negative comments such as "Pay attention!" "Sit up!" and were given fewer opportunities to read. McNeil feels that being taught in a negative, punishing way affects their learning.

A study done by J.N. Polardy found that boys whose teachers didn't believe in sex differences in reading skills read better than boys taught by teachers who believed that girls are better readers than boys. Teachers who are not sex-biased are more likely to produce students who don't show the learning weaknesses that the sexes are supposed to have.

Elementary school boys receive lower grades than girls, even though they score the same on IQ tests; but, as Stan found out, that changes as children get older. By junior high the boys have started to catch up, and by the end of high school girls have dropped considerably behind boys. What does the hidden curriculum do to girls?

When girls go to school, they've already been affected by sex-role stereotyping. Teachers expect the girls to be quieter and better behaved than boys. The teacher walks by as the girl is working and tells her what a nice, neat paper she has. With a satisfied smile, the girl promises herself to try hard tomorrow to have a nice, neat paper. She likes the approval of the teacher and finds that by being quiet and working hard she gets that approval. The sex stereotype is reinforced again and again.

When girls don't perform well, they are criticized for doing poor work. They don't get the encouragement and recognition for their efforts that boys do. Girls receive praise most often when they do well; therefore, they tend to hide their weaknesses. They don't like to risk taking on something they aren't sure of. Most girls avoid academic challenge that carries a possibility of failure and loss of teacher approval. As a result, they give up the possibility of intellectual growth that comes with stretching and risking.

The obedient, passive behavior that teachers praise in girls is the very thing that keeps girls from reaching their potential. Being neat, sitting still, doing your work, and doing as you are told have nothing to do with intellectual growth, curiosity, problem-solving, or the ability to cope with new situations and concepts. For teacher praise and good grades, seven-year-old girls give up the courage that it takes to conquer new and difficult material.

Avoidance of challenging situations, fear of failure, and passive behavior that is reinforced by teacher approval can actually cause a decline in ability. Maccoby's research showed that children whose IQs will likely increase are competitive, self-assertive, independent, and dominant in interaction with other children. The children who are likely to show a decline in IQ between ages six and ten are those who are passive, shy, and dependent. In the traditional primary classroom, the former describes boys, and the latter, girls. By praising and reinforcing sex-role behavior, schools may be limiting or even decreasing female students' ability.

THE HIDDEN CURRICULUM AND SELF-ESTEEM

Somewhere in the lessons of the hidden curriculum is the message that boys are better than girls. One hundred boys and girls eight to fifteen were asked to rate whether girls or boys had a greater degree of each of nineteen desirable and fourteen undesirable traits. As children grew older, their opinions of girls declined and they thought more highly of boys. More power and prestige are given to the male role. When such high value is put on the masculine role, females are viewed as inferior. Schools reinforce that idea.

Boys are given more leadership roles than girls. When something is to be carried, teachers are more likely to ask two boys to carry it, even though the girls in fifth grade are usually bigger than the boys. Books show pictures of boys and girls together, and the boys are taller than the girls, even though young boys are usually shorter than girls.

With the help of laws and women who have worked hard to make changes, school texts are beginning to be less sexist. When Stan was in elementary school he saw the stereotypic male-female, mother-father, boys do all the exciting things and girls play "little Suzy homemaker" in his reading texts. History told of Betsy Ross, who was in a nice feminine role sewing the flag, but was seriously lacking in reference to other women. Carrie Nation got a few lines for chopping down doors in her battles for temperance, but the battle for women's rights was hardly whispered. Woman suffrage was over when they won the right to vote—all fixed, no more problems. There was no time to talk about women. "Real" history had to be covered, and men made all the "real" history.

Girls looking for an inspiring model in history books,

biographies, and fiction may be very disappointed in how few there are. Teachers who reinforce sex roles don't provide a nonsexist model for girls. Boys on the other hand have role models in school. The likelihood is overwhelming that a male principal is looked on as the boss of the school and the teacher. Often there are male teachers who are valued more than female teachers. In one study teachers themselves, both female and male, said they believed that children preferred to be taught by a man rather than a woman. Besides role models at school, boys also have textbooks, biographies, and fiction for inspiration and reassurance that the future will bring success.

The message is loud and clear. Females are not as good as males, not as important, not as valuable, not as successful in the "real" world, and not capable or competent.

Self-esteem comes from feelings of confidence, capability, and worth. Fear of failure, of disapproval, of not being able to handle new and difficult situations eats away at self-esteem. Seeing boys get leadership roles, do all the "technical" things like run the VCR (even though the girls may do it at home), have most of the active roles in books, and grow up to be the boss or the rescuer of females reminds girls that boys are better, are superior. The reverse is true for girls. Girls are not as good as boys, girls should be subservient to men, and girls are inferior. That belief does not promote self-esteem. Stan may have thought that it wasn't exactly devaluing females, but if you put emphasis and value on one sex, the other is being devalued.

Because of the hidden curriculum, children are not developing to their unique potential. Their options are restricted, and their view of their place in the world is narrowed. They can't appreciate each other fully, nor can they appreciate themselves as complete human beings.

Developing potential, exploring options, having a broader view of the world, and appreciating self and others can be encouraged in the schools but will require getting rid of the hidden curriculum.

CHAPTER ◇ 4

High School Sexism

P utting down her pen, Pam Chee thanked Stan for filling her in on what he'd found out about sexism in elementary schools. "I read a little about elementary schools. Then I read how sexism in high schools causes girls to lower their expectations. I knew that was what I wanted to do for my part of the project."

"I'm anxious to hear what you found out. Does it go along with my information?" Stan wanted to know.

"It sure does," Pam assured him. "Actually, it gets worse as we grow older. When I say 'we', I mean females. You mentioned that girls' progress slows as they get older. I wondered why that happens. Some studies just give it as a fact, but others offer some explanations. From my own experience I tend to agree with the researchers who believe that sex-role stereotyping has a lot to do with it."

"What's your theory?" Stan asked.

"Well, I think it's a combination of things. Peer pressure is one factor. You know, Stan, it's not just pressure to drink or do drugs that we hear so much about. It has to do with being accepted by others. Girls are programmed from day one to seek approval. In high school the need for approval becomes overwhelming. The need for adult approval isn't as important, but peer approval is vital to most of us. Then the whole sexuality issue raises its ugly head. Our self-esteem gets all hung up in how we look and whether we're attractive to boys."

"Wait a minute," Stan interrupted. "Isn't that going a little overboard?"

Pam shook her head emphatically. "No, I don't think so. When I first started my research, I thought the whole sexism thing was exaggerated. I didn't know anything about sex-role stereotyping. I didn't know where to begin until I talked to Ms. Arthur at the library. She gave me a short article on the development of sex roles and recommended a book on sexism in schools. I skimmed through until I came to a chapter on the high school years. At first, like you, I thought it was exaggerated. It said, among other things, that sex-role stereotyping causes high school girls to believe that how they look and attracting boys are the most important things in life. I thought that was stupid. While I was sitting there thinking how stupid it was, I heard two girls behind me talking. Do I need to tell you what they were talking about?" Shaking her head and rolling her eyes upward, Pam paused.

"Well, that doesn't prove anything. That's just one instance," Stan said.

"It sure got me looking and listening, though. And you know what I found out, Stan? We can't get away from the stereotype. We're bombarded with 'You gotta look good and you gotta have a boyfriend.' You see the ads on TV. Have you ever looked at the magazines girls read? All the ads are about looking good so you can have a boyfriend. Use this makeup or wear that outfit and you'll be irresist-ible. If you don't have a boyfriend, you're a dog. And it's because you aren't wearing the right clothes or makeup. I saw an ad for class rings with the caption, 'The class ring too good to get in class.' The ring was on a girl's hand, which was, of course, held by a boy's hand."

"The ads always have guys who are good-looking and have great bodies. They're with beautiful women. It works the same way for guys. I don't see what that has to do with school achievement?" asked Stan, looking puzzled.

"For some girls it's more important to have a boyfriend than to do well in school. I heard a friend of Mom's tell her, 'I ask Traci what happened at school, and I get a rundown on what happened at lunch.' Of course, what happened at lunch had to do with boys. If you're going to keep a boy happy, you can't be too smart or better than he is in anything. Boys have to be better. You said you found that out in your research, Stan.

"Girls pretend to be dumb sometimes. If they don't, they don't get many dates," Pam went on. "Males feel threatened by women who are very bright and self-confident. I wanted to check that out, so I talked to three women who I think are intelligent. One is in college, one is about thirty and married, and the third is older and divorced. They all said the same thing. They know that they intimidate most men. The one in college said that in high school she played dumb sometimes to get boys to take her out. The one who's thirty said she did, too, but if she went out with a guy she had to play dumb with, he was boring. The older woman said that in her twenties she met a guy she had been interested in. He told her he had been interested in her but knew she was too smart for him to snow. That's why he had never asked her out. Women of all ages are playing dumb to keep men feeling good, and to keep men, period!"

"Whew, Pam, that's what my English teacher would call a sweeping generalization," Stan said. "I'll have to think about that. I'm not sure whether I don't like it because it isn't true or because it is. You know, though, women keep that stereotype going when they play the game."

"I agree completely, Stan," Pam said. "Boys have their stereotypes to deal with, too. If girls think they have to play dumb so guys can be better, guys must really be under pressure to *be* better."

With an emphatic nod, Stan agreed. He told Pam his feelings about being expected to live up to the macho idea of masculinity. She hadn't considered that boys had pressures for attracting girls. As they talked, they both realized that they judged a boy by how attractive his girlfriend was. Girls didn't necessarily have to go with good-looking boys as long as the boys were popular or good in sports or somehow were acceptable to others, or at least to their particular peer group. After they had talked about how sex roles influence relationships, Stan summed it up by saying, "So that's why you think sex-role stereotypes force a girl into building up a guy's ego at the expense of her own?"

"That's one part of what happens to girls," Pam said. "This whole thing about boys doing better in math and science is another part. Isn't it interesting that boys get lower grades than girls in elementary school but suddenly get so smart in junior high and high school. One researcher had a theory about that. With all the focus on the "feminizing" in the elementary schools and the damage done to boys, girls have been left out. What actually happens is that boys receive better teaching. You found that out, Stan. That's why boys can catch up in junior high. If boys can catch up in general achievement through better teaching, why can't girls keep up with boys in math and science through more attention and better teaching?"

"Are you asking me?" It was plain from his tone of voice that Stan wasn't about to offer any theories of his own.

"Well, not really." Pam smiled. "I didn't mean to get so excited. It's just that this is so new to me, and I'm feeling kind of ripped off. The whole idea of gender-appropriate subjects has kind of gotten to me, too. I can see where I've stayed away from some classes because they're considered masculine. I feel dumb in math and science, but why can't I do well in them if I do well in everything else? I can see where sex-role stereotyping has hung me up. I've thought that it's okay if I'm not good in math and science because girls aren't supposed to be. Now I'm beginning to think that maybe I've been programmed to feel thay way. Anyhow, it's got me looking at myself a little differently."

"You know, Pam, boys do the same thing. I think it would be good to know shorthand for taking notes in college, but I'm not going to sign up for shorthand when no other guys take it."

"Tell you what," Pam said with a grin, "I'll take calculus if you'll sign up for shorthand." They both laughed, and Pam went on. "What courses we sign up for can depend on our counselors, too. I might not have taken some of the classes that I did if Mr. Garrett hadn't told me that I could handle the challenge. Mom told me that her high school counselor talked her out of taking physics. He said she had a good grade point, and she might mess it up if she took physics. I don't think any of our counselors do that, but I'll bet they still do in some schools."

"I can see that a counselor who's hung up on sex roles and gender-appropriate behavior could really mess somebody up," Stan remarked.

"Oh, another thing," Pam began. "Career counselors can open options for students or close them. Some schools have Career Day for juniors and seniors. How the day is organized and students prepared for it can make a big difference in the choices students make. I remember that all the construction industry jobs like carpenters, plumbers, and electricians had men in the booths. They didn't try to talk to girls to let us know that women are working in those jobs. They make good money, too. My sister has a friend, Karen, whose father is an electrical contractor. He hired Karen as a laborer. She's a journeyman, now, and her father believes she's serious. He's planning to teach her about the business, and she expects to take it over eventually. Girls need to know about women like Karen. And when Career Day is planned, there ought to be women in all the booths."

"I agree," Stan said. "And I'd like to see men in the booths for nursing schools and secretarial schools. There's another thing I wanted to ask you about, Pam. We agreed that you'd do the textbook part of the project. Remember?"

"Oh, yeah. Thanks for reminding me. Most of the studies on textbooks were done in the seventies, but there wasn't a lot of progress in the eighties. History is still 'his story.' Women aren't shown in a bad light in history texts, they're just not shown. Texts include a few women, but most women are still left out or mentioned as extensions of men. The books say things like: 'The pioneers took their families on the long journey west.' When Marie Curie is mentioned, they always say that she worked with her husband. There are some supplemental books on women in history; if you have a teacher who's interested you may get some of it. We haven't had anything, I know. Colleges offer women's studies courses. If you don't take the courses, you don't get to know about the contributions women have made in history and are making today.

"Publishers have been slow doing anything about sexism in textbooks because it's so expensive to revise them, especially if their books are used by many school systems. They're making lots of money with the texts as they are.

Some states are beginning to refuse texts because of sexism, and publishers see money lost if they don't change. Some publishers have issued guidelines on treatment of women and minorities to make authors aware of sexism in their writing. You know, Stan, my dad says everything always comes down to dollars and cents. Anyway, it looks as if more districts will have to demand nonsexist texts before anything significant is done."

"I was curious about elementary school readers," Stan said, "so I asked my little sister and her friends what women do in their books. All of them said that the mothers cleaned the house and cooked and stuff. Maybe the books do show women outside of the stereotypes, but my sister and her friends aren't noticing. That may be because of their own sex-role thinking, but I think it says something about the books, too."

"They may not be using new books," Pam suggested. "Even though books are available that aren't so sexist, it doesn't mean schools have them. If schools have the books, teachers may not use them. I think most teachers do in our school. They're glad to get new texts. But some teachers like the old books. Mr. Williams uses the old algebra books. He says they're better than the new ones."

"I know a couple of teachers who use the old books because they don't want to have to make lesson plans and tests for the new books," Stan declared with a scowl.

"Besides textbooks, we have reading lists for English. Teachers have used the same lists forever. I know some of the books are classics and all that, but it doesn't mean we should ignore the fact that they reinforce the sex-role stereotypes," Pam asserted. "I think teachers should discuss how sexist the books are. They should point out the stereotyping. If the women are weak or airheads, that should be talked about. It seems they're either weak or airheaded or nagging and awful. Look at the stereotyping in Shakespeare's *Taming of the Shrew*. We've read other plays by him that are really sexist.

"I've been thinking about something else, too," Pam said. "Title IX of the Education Amendment of 1972 that went into effect July 21, 1975, states: 'No person in the United States shall, on the basis of sex, be excluded from participation in, be denied the benefits of, or be subjected to discrimination under any education program or activity receiving federal assistance.' That means that anybody can be in any class or any activity. That's why our P.E. classes are mixed—or at least we have a male and female teacher for each class. Some of the activities we do together. We all do archery, but we don't play team sports together. Once in a while we play mixed volley ball.

"I asked Ms. Hall about that, and she said that for P.E. there's a 'separate but equal' clause in the law. So our school provides separate but equal activities. I'm not sure I agree with that."

"What don't you agree with?" Stan asked.

"I don't think all activities are equal."

"You use the same equipment and play on the same fields and courts," Stan reminded her.

"Oh, yeah, we play on the same field. The boys get the diamond with the infield and pitcher's mound, and we go out in the corner and make our own softball diamond."

"Well, a softball diamond is shorter than a baseball diamond. You can't use the diamond anyway," was Stan's defense.

"Then why don't we have a softball diamond equal to your baseball diamond to play on?"

Stan had no answer for that. Nor could he answer why the boys' basketball team had newer uniforms and more equipment than the girls'. Pam refused to accept the money-making factor of boys' sports as a reason for short-changing the girls' program. The girls had championship basketball and volleyball teams. Given the opportunity to have Friday night games, Pam thought they could bring in a paying crowd, too.

"It seems to me that a lot of things are separate but *not* equal in our school. I'm beginning to think I've missed out on a lot because I bought the stereotypes for so long. I haven't been taught about women who are intelligent, courageous, important, or even real human beings. I've been told I'm dumb in math and science, that attracting males is my main purpose, that if I'm smart I shouldn't be too smart. Nobody expects very much of me, so I don't have to expect too much of myself. Stan, I bought this stuff and I'm feeling ripped off and mad."

"I don't think our school is as bad as lots of schools," Stan objected. In fact, some things show real progress. I guess what bothers me is that nobody talks about it. Nobody talks about the sex-role stereotyping in *Wuthering Heights* or *Great Expectations*. Nobody mentions the sex-role stereo-types in Shakespeare. We need to talk about that stuff. Even if that was the way things were then, we don't have to say it was okay. It wasn't okay then, and it isn't okay now."

"So women have been left out of history in the past. We don't have to let that keep happening. Stan, there's got to be something we can do to change things."

"You know, Pam, I have a feeling that this project has started things moving in that direction. Our meeting tomorrow should be something else. When you women get together, there's no telling what'll happen."

Stan's comment broke Pam's intensity, and she laughed. When she left, she felt that she had clarified a lot in her own mind. She also knew that she didn't want to drop things where they were. She definitely wanted to do something. Talking with the rest of the group might give her some ideas for bringing about change.

SEX-ROLE STEREOTYPING AT SCHOOL

Young people today are becoming more aware of their responsibility for their world. Pam wants to do something to change what she sees keeping young people, particularly young women, from realizing their potential. Because they accept the sex-role stereotypes, young women lower expectations for themselves. There's a progressive building to that from the early grades.

At first, girls outperform boys in school. Sitting still and doing what adults want has already brought them much success and approval.

Boys generally are more aggressive than girls. Because of their rowdy behavior, teachers spend a lot of time interacting with them. Boys don't get as much feedback about their academic performance as they do about their behavior. Although girls receive less negative feedback, the criticism is usually about their academic work. As a result, girls generally associate poor academic performance with a lack of ability. A lack of ability is something you can't control. If you think you lack ability, you question your capability.

When boys receive criticism for poor performance, they're encouraged to try harder. "You can do it," is the message they receive. Girls hear only that they can't do it. Over time, girls tend to believe that they're less likely to succeed because they think of themselves as less capable than boys.

As Pam and Stan discovered, boys begin to outperform girls academically in the junior high years. The pressure to succeed becomes greater as they grow older. By high school, boys are feeling the pressure to work hard so they can have a successful career. They're already being prepared for the role of breadwinner.

According to the sex-role stereotypes, girls will not have to support a family so they don't need to worry about succeeding in school or in a career. If you believe the stereotype, you believe that girls are not good in math and science. They are not skillful with their hands and are not likely to be interested in learning such skills. The stereotype says that girls are less logical, and their analytic skills are inferior to males. Their interest in careers is not serious or long term because their lives will be centered around home and family. That is a very limiting stereotype.

Without realizing what she had bought into, Pam had accepted that stereotype. She lowered her expectations for herself and thought nothing of it. When young women believe the stereotypes, they allow them to control their lives. You can't do what you don't believe you can. Pam's anger and feeling of being cheated may motivate her to change her expectations of herself and go after what she wants. She could see that the choices she was making about courses to take now would influence her choice of career later.

Looking at subjects and jobs as gender-appropriate narrows the options for both young women and young men. When Pam and Stan talked about Career Day, they could immediately see possibilities for showing more options to young people. Today the gender gap is being bridged in many fields. It still isn't easy to cross the gender lines in many occupations, but more and more women and men are accepting the challenge.

When Title IX of the Education Amendments of 1972 became effective, women across the country were encouraged. However, change has been very slow. Even though the law bars discrimination in any education program or activity, young women have had to fight for the right to equal opportunity in school. Many young people, female and male, accept the sexist rules of schools regarding male-only or female-only classes because they don't know that such rules are illegal. They allow themselves to be counseled out of subjects they want to take because counselors want them to take gender-appropriate classes. Under Title IX such things are clearly not allowed. If you would like to know more about Title IX, write to Project on Equal Education Rights (PEER), 1112 13th Street NW, Washington, D.C. 20005. Ask for publications on *Title IX Resources*: #017-080-01710-5, "A Student Guide to Title IX," and #017-080-1671-1, "Identifying Discrimination."

Many states have Title IX offices in their education department. Large school districts usually have someone who is in charge of Title IX issues. Women's organizations are also interested in school compliance with Title IX.

A glaring area of noncompliance is sports. Pam mentioned the separate but equal ruling. Very few schools put as much money into the girls' sports program as into the boys'. The claim that male sports bring in money to support the female programs was found to be untrue in a Senate investigation. More than 90 percent of the so-called revenue-producing sports actually cost the schools more money than they bring in. Student body fees make up the difference, and half of those fees are paid by female students!

Schools are supposed to have sex-integrated physical education classes and teams, with two exceptions. Contact sports may be sex-segregated, and teams and classes may be single-sex if they turn out that way because of ability grouping. Schools use that part of the law in many ways to avoid change and exclude girls from teams for which they are skilled and qualified.

The progress in eliminating sexism in schools is slow and will probably continue to be, but there are ways you can become part of the solution to the problem.

WHAT YOU CAN DO

Often young people feel helpless about changing anything in the school system. Sometimes students try to take things into their own hands and force the school to change. It's always best to work through available social structures. Many civil rights activists of the 1960s ran for political office in the late '70s and '80s. They realized that they would be listened to and would be more likely to effect change by being part of the system. Look at some ways you might use the system to bring about change.

Adults are always good resources. If you are concerned about textbooks in your school, ask a teacher or counselor you feel comfortable with how books are chosen. Talk about your concerns. There may be a committee in your school district that would be interested in your comments. Having an adult refer you to the group will help you be taken seriously. It's important to remember that you don't want housewives out of textbooks; you want female plumbers and surgeons in.

Now that you're aware of the effect that sexism has on your education, you are also more aware of teachers who are trying to do something about sexism. Those teachers can be a wonderful resource. Perhaps one would be willing to sponsor a women's awareness discussion group. Perhaps one belongs to a women's organization and could tell you how to get literature and talk with you about issues that concern you.

If you can't find someone in your school to help you, look in the Yellow Pages of your phone directory under Women's Organizations or Associations. Call or write those groups and ask if they have education committees. You'll be warmly welcomed.

Your library is another valuable resource. The librarian can direct you to listings of organizations interested in nonsexist education. PEER, at the address listed above, has materials in all areas of education. Take the time to write letters and get information.

Your community college, college, or university is a good source of information. Most schools have a department or office of women's studies or a women's resource center. Ask for a reading list and share the list with your English teacher.

Talking about sexism when you see it and experience it is very important. Pam's observation that no one talks about it is a good point. If you don't call attention to sexism, it will be ignored as an issue and maintained as a result. Talk to your teachers. If a teacher or counselor is sexist, consider letting the person know your feelings. Chapter 5 suggests some ways to confront people appropriately. Find a teacher, counselor, or other adult with whom you can discuss sexism at school. Bring the issue into the open.

Talk to your parents about your concerns. If it is difficult for you to talk to them, talk to a friend's parents or a neighbor who will discuss the subject with you. Talk to your friends. The fact that it got them talking is an important result of the project Pam and Stan and the others are doing. They're exchanging information and ideas. Change doesn't happen without exchange.

All change starts with you. If you wait for the world to

change, it will never happen. When your attitudes, ideas, beliefs, and perceptions about yourself change, your world will begin to change.

Young women must stop considering themselves merchandise on the market to attract young men. That doesn't mean that you must go around looking as unattractive as possible. There's nothing wrong with wanting to look your best. The way you dress and the way you look are important to you, but examine how important they are. It's normal and natural to be interested in boys. Having a relationship with a man is a wonderful part of life. How important is having a boyfriend to you? What do you do to keep a boyfriend? Ask yourself if you have bought into the sex-role stereotype of the "typical high school girl." Have you turned away from independence, intelligence, and assertiveness to be feminine and attractive so you can appeal to "Mr. Right" who will make your world complete? You may be sacrificing your ability and talent in order to fulfill the traditional feminine sex role.

Young men must look at the sex-role stereotypes they have accepted. Have you given up your feelings to "be a man"? Do you have to be tough to be accepted? When you're sad and cry, do you feel shame? Is it difficult to appreciate a female who is more talented or more intelligent than you? Do confident, independent women make you uncomfortable? Would you play tennis with a girl who beat you eight times out of ten? Ten times out of ten? Would you feel the same way about a girl outscoring you in a basketball game as you do about a boy? Consider your answers to these questions, you may be carrying a heavy load of sex-role stereotyping. You may be giving up part of your "humanhood" to maintain your "manhood."

CHAPTER 5

Speaking of Sexism

"**A**lex, you're making life difficult for me," Chris said as she sat down on the bench at the bus stop.

"What are you blamin' me for now?" Alex Richards demanded from the post he was leaning against.

"You're the one who said that equal time had to be given to the sexist things that are said about men. I can find all kinds of things that women have written about sexist language directed at women, but it's hard to find stuff on the other side. I'm having to listen and look for stuff myself, and I hate it."

"All right!" Alex cheered. "But I don't see what's so bad about that."

"You would if it was your own stuff you had to look at," Chris replied. "What I'm finding out is that some women say things that are just as prejudiced and sexist about men as men say about women. I have to include myself in some of it, too.

"When I took the part on sexist language, I thought it would be easy. This whole thing started because Mr. Crawford called me 'honey' and a 'cute little thing' in that nasty, suggestive, put-down tone of voice. I thought I had this language thing all taken care of. Then you had to demand equal time and get me thinking about female sexists."

"Oh, this is great!" crowed Alex. "You women are just as bad as men. You do the same thing to men that men do to women."

"Just hang on a minute, man. I didn't say that. Sure we say some sexist things about men. My favorite bumper sticker is 'The best man for the job is a woman.' But I'm thinking more about how women put down women. It's really gotten complicated."

"You know, Chris, everybody I talk to says the same thing. This project is really making us think. What's so complicated about what you're doing?"

"I guess it's that it isn't just men hassling women and putting them down. There's more to it than that. I was talking to Gina on the phone yesterday, and we got into the thing about men being the authority and males being valued more in society than females. That goes back to the beginning of time. The whole thing is rooted in history. Remember how the Greeks and the Romans disregarded women? The men were everything. Women weren't considered much better than slaves. The whole struggle for recognition as human beings worthy of consideration has taken centuries."

"Oh c'mon, Chris."

"It's true, Alex. Listen to this." Chris took a paper out of her notebook and began reading quotes to Alex. "Pythagoras said, 'There is a good principle which created order, light, and man, and an evil principle which created chaos, darkness, and woman.' And listen to this one from Cato the Elder in 195 B.C. 'Suffer women once to arrive at an equality with you, and they will from that moment become your superiors.' By all means, let's keep those women in their place.

"You know what that great Christian leader Martin Luther said? 'God created Adam lord of all living creatures, but Eve spoiled it all.' Napoleon had a few goodies to throw our way too. 'Nature intended women to be our slaves...they are our property; we are not theirs They belong to us, just as a tree that bears fruit belongs to the gardener. What a mad idea to demand equality for women! ...Women are nothing but machines for producing children.'"

"All right, already," Alex broke in. "You've made your point."

"Oh, don't you want to hear the more modern ones like Rudyard Kipling, who said, 'A woman is only a woman, but a good cigar is a smoke.' That from a literary genius. And how about that master of the human mind Sigmund Freud. He said, 'The great question that has never been answered, and which I have not yet been able to answer despite my thirty years of research into the feminine soul, is: What does a woman want?' David Susskind, the producer of the 1987 TV series on great men, said, 'There are no great women.' And Bob Knepper, the Houston Astros pitcher, didn't like female umpires because, according to him, 'Women were created in a role of submission to men and should not be in a position of leadership.'"

As Alex started to protest, Chris held up her hand and said, "Just one more. This from Abbie Hoffman, that great radical political leader of the '60s, who with six others went to jail for standing up for his rights. 'The only alliance I would make with the Women's Liberation Movement is in bed.' Since forever, Alex, it's been men are better than women and women are only good for sex."

"You know, Chris, when you start hammering, you don't

use a sledge hammer; you use a pile driver. I see where you're coming from."

"The thing is, Alex, it's still going on. The sexist remarks that women make about men are a way of fighting back, of getting even. Things like 'When God made man, She was only joking.' That gets even for the Eve comments and jokes."

"That makes sense," Alex granted, "but it doesn't make it any less sexist."

Chris agreed, and then Alex wanted to know what she meant about women putting down women. Taking another paper from her notebook, Chris said, "These are some things that women have said about women, and just recently, too. Tracy Ullman said, 'I don't have much respect for other women and much prefer men. Men don't gossip or get catty, and most of my friends are men.' When Diane Sawyer substituted for Dan Rather on CBS News, TV critic Kay Gardella said, 'I still like getting my nightly news from a man...during her [Sawyer's] sub stint for Dan Rather on Tuesday night, I felt like something was missing.' Women putting down women makes it even harder to get rid of the stereotypes."

"I see your point, Chris. You know, there's something I've been wondering about ever since our first meeting when you were so mad at Mr. Crawford for calling you 'honey.' Dad calls my mother 'Hon' and 'Love' and stuff like that, and she calls him 'Honey' and 'Darling.' What's wrong with that?"

"Your Mom and Dad are special to each other. When they call each other 'Hon' it means they care about each other. When Mr. Crawford called me 'Honey' it made me a nonperson. He looked at me like...like...like a sex object. I felt dirty. There are times when people 'Honey' me and I feel nonexistent. It's just a word that doesn't mean anything. And other times I know I'm being called 'Honey' because I'm not considered important. I'm being talked down to. What's the word? Um . . . patronized. That's it. I feel patronized."

"But people don't always mean it that way," Alex protested.

"Well, maybe they need to become more conscious of what they're doing."

"Aw, c'mon, Chris. Old Mrs. Whitfield calls everybody 'Darlin'.' You gonna raise her consciousness?"

Chris laughed. "All right, point taken. Mrs. Whitfield is an old dear, and I wouldn't think of changing her, okay? But words are important. You wouldn't like being called a 'wimp'." As Alex's expression told her that he didn't like it at all, she asked, "What does 'wimp' mean to you?"

"You'd just as well call me a 'woman' as call me a 'wimp'," Alex said.

"Oh, that's even better. Now tell me in words what that means."

"Well, it's like being called weak . . . feminine . . . not a man . . . uh . . . you know," Alex struggled.

"Yeah, it insults your manhood. It's as bad as calling you 'gay' or 'queer'. You don't want to be like that lower form, woman." As Alex started to protest, Chris said, "Think about it, Alex. It comes down to males are better than females. I heard you tell Paul that Colleen is just like one of the guys on the soccer team. I've seen you out with the girls' volleyball team after a game you refereed for them. How would you like it if they told someone you were just like one of the girls on the team?"

Paul opened his mouth, changed his mind, and closed it.

"For Colleen it's a compliment to be one of the guys because being male is better than being female. It's even better for females to be more like males."

"You've given me a lot to think about, Chris. I'm working on media and entertainment, and I can see that some stuff I thought was stupid isn't as stupid as I thought."

Alex saw his bus coming and said, "Here I go. I'll see you Wednesday at the meeting."

After Alex left, Chris looked over her notes and thought how powerful words are. If you say a man is aggressive, it means he's ambitious, but an aggressive woman is "pushy" or "uppity." If a man is forgetful, he's absentminded, but a woman is scatterbrained. If a man is talkative he's being sociable, whereas a woman would be accused of gossiping. A woman who is argumentative is an agitator, but a man would be described as persistent or competitive. If a man isn't married, people congratulate him on his ability to avoid "getting caught." If a woman isn't married, it's assumed there's something wrong with her. She must be some kind of social or sexual reject.

The more Chris thought about it, the more she wanted to do something about it. She wanted to make changes in herself, and she wanted to make others aware so they could change some of the things they said, too. By the time her bus came, she had decided to work on her own stuff first. As she rode home, Chris thought of two things she wanted to do. First, she would work on the sexist things she said and thought. She put in thought because she didn't always call a person a "wimp," but she thought it a lot. She had to admit that she thought it about girls too. Second, she wanted to be able to say something back when sexist comments were made around her. Chris had seen the book *Coping Through Assertiveness* by Rhoda McFarland in the library when she was doing her research. She decided to check it out and see if it would help her handle the sexist comments.

When she got off at her stop, Chris felt good about what

she had to report to the group on Wednesday, and she felt good about what she had decided to do for herself.

THE LANGUAGE OF SEXISM

The generic term for human beings is man, and it's a man's world. If people were referred to as "womankind," would it seem strange? Would men feel included? How would you feel if you heard a great world leader say, "All women are sisters" or "We all share in the sisterhood of woman?" How about a Christmas message that says "Peace on earth, good will to women?" Did the writers of the Declaration of Independence mean to leave out women when they said "All men are created equal"?

"Don't be silly," say those who don't take sexism seriously or who want to keep sex-role stereotypes. "Women know they're included when 'man' is used generically." When children first hear "man" used meaning universal man, girls have to be told to include themselves but boys know they're included. Chris and Gina were right when they decided that sexist thinking is rooted in the belief that men are better than women, that male characteristics are more desirable than female, that men are more valuable than women. Throughout history, that has made it okay for men and women to devalue and discount women.

THE DEVALUED WOMAN

Being called "honey" made Chris feel less than a person. She had become like every other female that Mr. Crawford didn't value very highly.

"Ms." is preferred as a title by many women because it gives them equal footing with men. "Mr." says "man," and you don't know if the man is married or not. His title isn't determined by his relationship to anyone else. "Miss" and "Mrs." designate a woman by her status relative to a man. "Mrs." tells you that she's taken by a man, and "Miss" lets you know that she's available for the taking. The individual woman has no status in and of herself.

By putting "woman" or "lady" before a word, you can make its status just a little less than it was without the qualifier, as in woman doctor, woman lawyer, ladies' golf tournament, women's tennis, girls' softball.

By saying Colleen was "just like the guys," Alex was giving her a compliment, raising her value. Being more like a male is acceptable to people. The opposite is not true. To devalue a male most effectively, you need only imply that he has female qualities, as Chris pointed out so well. It is immediately taken to reflect on his "manhood" and suggests homosexuality.

WOMAN, THE OBJECT

"Cute little thing" in a suggestive tone made Chris feel dirty. When a boy at school mentioned the locker room talk to her, he blushed. Males refer to females by many slang expressions—"chick," "broad," "bimbo," "babe." All of those words treat females as objects, things, not human beings. A survey of college students showed that college males know twice as many slang terms for women as women do, and almost all of them are sexual. Surveys made to find words for sexually active males and females revealed 220 for females and 22 for males. There are 220 ways to insult, dishonor, discredit, and degrade females.

To be something to be gotten "a piece of" doesn't give one much status as a human being. A woman is degraded and objectified through her sexuality. A man is praised for his sexuality. When he "gets the piece," he's more of a man, and the woman is put down. The way to degrade a man is to suggest homosexuality. There aren't nearly as many words to do that as there are to degrade a woman.

THE DISAPPEARING WOMAN

Language can make women disappear. More and more women are keeping their birth name when they marry or adding their husband's name with a hyphen. If you wonder why, you might ask yourself why a man wouldn't want to give up his name and take his wife's name. Forget the fact that it's the custom for women to give up their birth name (another sexist men-are-more-important-than-women custom). Consider why men wouldn't give up their name. One major reason is that he would give up his identity. A woman is expected to be proud to be Mrs. James Phillips, but a man wouldn't want to be Mr. Angela West. He wouldn't even want to be part of the couple Mrs. and Mr. Angela West. And wouldn't it be awful to read in the paper that the Angela Wests are touring Europe? What happened to Jim? Did he just disappear? Angela may feel that she doesn't want to disappear when she marries Jim. She may decide to keep her birth name.

WOMEN AND SEXIST LANGUAGE

There may not be as many slang words for putting men down, but women know how to do it well. Since the way to insult men is to suggest homosexuality, anything that reflects on their "manhood" will do the trick. Little boys are called "sissy" and men are called "wimp," "limp-wrist," "weakling," "lightweight," or "fem." A woman may not call a man a weakling to his face, but she'll tell her friends what she thinks of him, using her own sexist terms.

With a little practice, you can be funny and not come right out and say a man is a "wimp." Molly Ivins did it very well in the November, 1988, issue of *MS* magazine. When someone predicted that Dan Quayle would bring women votes to the Republican ticket because of his good looks, Ms. Ivins wrote about the soon to be Vice President, "Actually Quayle looks exactly like Princess Di..." Alex would be happy to know that Chris would consider that a sexist comment.

Some women lump men into one big stereotyped blob and say things like, "You know how men are. He can't do a thing for himself," or "Well, what can you expect of a man? You know they never do what they say they will," or "Men are like children. They never grow up." It is a way of saying that women are better than men. This common attitude is demonstrated in a cartoon in the June, 1988, issue of *MS* magazine. The woman character says, "Men have to be *trained.* They come to you in *a rough state* to be *molded and shaped* into a *pleasant, civilized* human being, worth spending the rest of your life with...by which time your life may well be OVER." There's an underlying belief that, although men may run the world, they couldn't do it without women.

Greeting cards can carry double meanings. One card read, "Happy Birthday to the man who wears the pants... from the woman who irons them." Half the message is, "You're the boss and I happily serve you." The other half says, "You may think you're the boss, but I know better." That's a nicely done put-down.

Sexists comments work both ways, as Alex pointed out. It's important to realize that sexism in any form is harmful to *people*, not just to *female* people.

Perhaps the sexist put-downs most harmful to women are those made by other women. Chris found the comments by Tracy Ullman and Kay Gardella very distressing. It was hard for her to understand their attitudes. If Chris remembers that women also believe in the sex-role stereotypes it will help her understand why some women say the sexist things they do.

Tracy Ullman obviously believes the stereotype, and her conversation reflects her belief. That doesn't excuse her, but it helps one to understand her. Besides hurting other women with her comments, she hurts herself. Since she has little respect for women, she can expect little respect for herself as a woman from the sexists she supports.

In her *MS* article, Molly Ivins scolds George Bush's sister, Nancy Bush Ellis, for her comments about Ann Richards's keynote address to the Democratic convention. Ms. Ellis said she thought it was "bitchy, catty, and demeaning to women." Ms. Ivins reminds Mrs. Ellis that bitchy and catty are "words used only to demean women." However, Ms. Ivins did a little demeaning on her own. The complete quote about Dan Quayle is, "Actually, Quayle looks like Princess Di, while Mrs. Quayle looks exactly like Prince Philip. What more could any woman want?" In one sentence both a man and a woman are devalued.

COPING WITH SEXIST LANGUAGE

An effective way to cope with sexist language is through assertiveness. Assertiveness is a way to take control of yourself and treat yourself and others with dignity and respect. When you're assertive, you take responsibility for your feelings, wants, and needs by making them known to others in ways that protect your rights and respect theirs.

Being assertive means being honest and direct about

what you're feeling. Chris felt insulted when Mr. Crawford spoke to her, but she didn't know how to tell him so. She was also very angry, but she didn't know how to express her anger without calling him names and shouting. Chris needed a way to take care of her feelings in an appropriate way. She needed to let Mr. Crawford know how she felt without giving up her personal dignity while she was about it. Through assertiveness she can express her feelings and protect her rights without harming others or infringing on their rights.

"I" MESSAGES

An "I" message allows you to state your feelings in a way that doesn't criticize, accuse, or blame others and doesn't put them down. With an "I" message you can state your feelings directly and honestly. "I feel insulted by that remark." "I'm really mad right now." With an "I" message you take complete responsibility for your feelings.

A "you" message is the opposite of an "I" message. "You make me mad" and "You insulted me" are "you" messages. They make the other person responsible for your feelings. With a "you" message there's always the temptation for name-calling and put-downs. "You make me mad, you chauvinist pig!"

Besides making the other person responsible for your feelings, a "you" message gives him or her power over you, power over your feelings. By saying, "I'm really angry," you keep your own power while letting the other person know you don't like the behavior. It also keeps the focus on the other person's behavior. A "you" message puts the other person on the defensive, and the natural response is to attack in return.

Chris: You really make me mad, Mr. Crawford.
          How dare you talk to me that way? You're
          nothing but a male chauvinist pig!"
Mr. C: Listen here, young lady, you watch your
          mouth. Show a little respect for your elders.
Chris: You didn't show any respect for me. You're
          insulting. I'm not your "honey."
Mr. C: You go on about your business. I give you a
          compliment and you act like I attacked you.

This little scene could go on with people getting more
and more angry. Mr. Crawford became the injured party
when Chris didn't treat him with dignity and respect. "I"
messages would have avoided the nastiness.

Chris: I feel insulted and put down when people
          call me "honey." My name is Chris.
Mr. C: Well, Chris, I certainly didn't mean to be
          insulting.
Chris: I feel real uncomfortable when people call
          me "a cute little thing." It makes me feel like
          I'm on display, like I'm being looked up and
          down.
Mr. C: There's nothing wrong with being appre-
          ciated.
Chris: I feel real uncomfortable, Mr. Crawford, and
          I feel angry too.
Mr. C: You don't have to get mad.
Chris: I just wanted you to know how I feel.

Chris has treated herself and Mr. Crawford with dignity
and respect. Mr. Crawford may not change his behavior,
but Chris has taken care of her feelings in an appropriate
way. Most of the time a simple "I" message will suffice.

Remember, "I feel that you insulted me," is a "you" message and very different from, "I feel insulted." The following "I" messages express feelings without attacking the other person.

"I feel put down when I'm called a 'chick.'"
"I feel uncomfortable when boys make comments about the way I walk."
"I feel insulted by that comment."
"I feel resentful when girls call me a chauvinist just because I'm a male."
"I feel annoyed when women make remarks about men that are as sexist as the ones they complain that men make."

You can express positive and negative feelings, say no, and let people know your wants and needs with "I" messages.

"I don't like to be called 'honey'."
"I don't want to be called 'a cute little thing'."
"I don't like being whistled at."
"I don't think comments like that are compliments."
"I don't go out with boys who call girls 'baby'."
"I don't want to be around when remarks like that are made."
"I don't appreciate sexist remarks from anyone."
"I want to be treated respectfully."
"I want the opportunity to be a lab assistant."
"I want to be judged on my ability, not my sex."
"I want to feel free to walk anywhere in school without being harassed because I'm female."
"I appreciate your nonsexist attitude."

"I admire your courage in standing up for your rights."

"I like the way you let her know that you don't like sexist remarks."

Using "I" messages keeps you in control of you, lets others know how you feel, and keeps the focus on the issue. You treat everyone, including yourself, with dignity and respect.

Chris wanted to make others aware of their sexist language so they could change. She wisely decided to change herself first. By changing yourself first, you'll find that other people become aware of their language too. When you respond to sexist comments assertively, you bring awareness to others. When you change yourself, you change the world around you as well. You have a positive effect by what you say and by what you no longer say. By stopping your sexist comments, the people you would have harmed, including yourself, are not hurt. When you let others know your feelings about their sexist language, you plant a seed for change. You may not think that you're accomplishing much, but big changes are the result of individuals making small changes.

CHAPTER 6

Sexism at Work

"**H**ey, Ellen, if you don't have to go right home, let's go to the Pit Stop for a Coke after school," Pam Chee called to Ellen Peterson as they passed in the hall on the way to their last-period classes. Ellen's okay came back as Pam turned the corner.

Later at the Pit Stop the girls talked about the English project. "When I was doing my research for sexism in the workplace," Ellen said, "I found out that sexism in school can have an important effect on our choice of job or career. That's what you've been saying. Women don't qualify for a lot of the technical jobs. It isn't because they're not smart enough; they just don't have the background. Women enter the data in computers, but men get the jobs in programming and systems analysis because of their math, science, and other technical training. Boys take the classes that give them the background they need for technical jobs. There are lots more boys than girls in our math, science, and computer science classes here."

"I've been thinking about that a lot the past few days," Pam said. "When I learned that girls fall behind in achievement in high school, I wondered if that were true here. I thought of the girls who were smart in elementary school but are average and not very interested in academics now. I talked to a couple of girls I know. From what they said, it looks as if they just lowered their expectations. They decided that they weren't going to go to college and have a career. They plan to work a few years after high school and then get married and have a family. They're locked into the sex-role stereotype."

"The bad part about that, Pam, is that wives make up over half the female workforce. Half of all mothers work outside the home. With the divorce rate what it is, you'd think that every female would realize that she will probably have to support herself and maybe her children for a good part of her life," Ellen said very solemnly. "My mother has told me ever since I can remember that she doesn't care what I decide to do; the important thing is to be able to take care of myself. She told me never to expect a man to provide for me all my life."

"Is that because she was divorced and had to work to support herself?" Pam asked.

"Partly," Ellen responded, "but she felt that way even before she got married. When she was fourteen, her father died suddenly. Her mother didn't have any special work skills because she was married right out of school. She took a liberal arts course and had no technical training at all. The company her father worked for gave her a job as a switchboard operator. Mom thinks the company felt sorry for my grandmother. Mom always says that you can't depend on anyone but yourself. I think she's right," Ellen said.

Pam agreed and said, "Women don't seem to realize how important it is to get training and education for higher-paying jobs."

"Sometimes we aren't encouraged in school to take the

classes that would prepare us for better jobs," Ellen said. "That isn't all, though. Women are discriminated against. They'll do the same work as a man, but the employer will give it a different job title and pay the woman less." After Pam's explosion at how unfair that was, Ellen went on to explain. "That's why it was made illegal. The law says that jobs that require approximately the same training, experience, responsibility, and skills should pay the same wages. It's called "comparable worth." Employers try to get around that, though, by saying that what the women do is not equal to what the men do. In one case a hospital was paying male orderlies more than female nurse's aides although their duties were almost the same. The case went to court, and the nurse's aides won.

"The Minnesota University system was sued by women employees whose salaries weren't comparable to men's. When the legislature checked to find out how much it would cost to defend the case, they discovered it would be cheaper to raise women's salaries than to go to court. One paper I read on the subject said that jobs will continue to be sex-segregated until the laws on discrimination and comparable worth are enforced."

"Haven't the laws been around a long time?" Pam asked. "It seems like it's taking a long time for things to change."

"Employers have been fighting it. They don't want to have to put out more money. Then in 1985 a ruling by the Equal Employment Opportunity Commission made things worse. They ruled that unequal pay for comparable jobs isn't proof of discrimination. The Equal Pay Act says that women must be paid the same as men when they do the same work, so they had to come up with a definition of 'same work'," Ellen said. "I have the definition somewhere in my notes, but it really is tight. The jobs have to be almost exactly the same and in the same place."

"There's another thing I've been wondering about," Pam commented. "So many jobs are considered women's jobs— you know, all the clerical jobs. The pay is really low. Why do those wages stay so low? Did you find out anything about that?" she asked.

Saying that the question was complicated, Ellen dug through her notes: "Here it is. This paper talks about wages and job segregation." She explained to Pam that when men and women do different jobs within an occupation, industry, or firm, it's called job segregation. Women who teach in colleges or universities are more likely to teach English. Men are more likely to teach engineering. In a large company the executives are more likely to be men and the secretaries women. Those are examples of job segregation."

Much job segregation is a result of choice. Women choose the sex-role-appropriate job that is lower-paying. Some people who have studied the problem think that married women cause the big differences in pay between men and women. Married women are more willing to take lower-paying positions than single or divorced women, and married women make up over half of the female workforce. However, to say that women choose jobs that conform to the sex role can be used against the interests of women who are struggling for equality. It makes it seem as though women don't want to get into more nontraditional jobs, which isn't true at all.

More women are going into nontraditional jobs, but the overall amount of sex segregation hasn't changed much since the early 1900s. From 1970 to 1985 there was a gain of 510,000 women in fields that were male-dominated. During the same period 3.3 million women joined the workforce as secretaries, nurses, bookkeepers, and cashiers, increasing the occupations that are female-dominated.

Some researchers say that job segregation will continue as long as jobs held by women receive lower pay. They also believe that until men enter a field it will remain underpaid. However, women entering an occupation in large numbers usually causes the wages to go down; then men leave the jobs.

"Women are rarely found in jobs with the highest pay and the best chance for advancement," Ellen said. "Even when women work in high-paying industries, their wages are usually less than men's."

"What about women who go into jobs that are nontraditional, like construction work?" Pam inquired.

"They can have a really hard time," Ellen said. "Sometimes the men won't have anything to do with them. Since there are no other women on the job, there's no support. It gets really lonely. Sometimes the men give them wrong information when they ask for help. They're harassed a lot, too; mostly through crude sexual remarks. You know what I mean. Now, though, more women are making complaints about sexual harassment when it happens. The laws that protect women in those situations and the laws that make it possible for women to be considered for those jobs are the result of the women's movement. Women have worked hard to get laws that give equal opportunity in the workplace."

"That brings up two things I wanted to ask you about," Pam said. "I want to talk about sexual harassment in a minute, but earlier you talked about discrimination, about discrimination in wages. When you talk about equal opportunity, doesn't that include other kinds of discrimination, too?"

"Oh, yeah, for sure," Ellen said. "There are all kinds of discrimination. The job title thing is one. Some companies have higher-paying positions with a very few women in them. For example, Sears stores had two categories of salespeople, those on straight salary and those on commissions. The people on commissions made a lot more. Men held 60 percent of the commissioned jobs and only 25 percent of the salaried jobs. The Equal Employment Opportunity Commission took them to court for discriminating against women. Sears said the jobs were open to women, but the women weren't applying for them. The court found in favor of Sears, but the EEOC appealed the case. The EEOC says that employers must make it clear that jobs are open to women whether women are applying for them or not.

"Another way employers discriminate," Ellen went on, "is by not promoting women. They claim that men don't want to work for women supervisors. Most men who say they don't want to work for women never have done so. Male managers claimed that they and other men and women wouldn't like female supervisors. When people who worked for women supervisors were asked, however, 75 percent said they liked working for their supervisor. Those same male managers asserted that women were not as reliable as men because of 'biological and personal characteristics.' They said that women leave jobs and are not dependable. Women leave low-paying clerical jobs when they aren't promoted. Men leave those same jobs even more often than women do. Women who have responsible jobs are just as dependable as men.

"The qualifications for a job can be rigged to keep women out," Ellen continued. "Alabama had a requirement that prison guards had to be five feet two inches tall and weigh one hundred twenty pounds. That may not look like discrimination, but 41 percent of all women are wiped out of that job before they start. Only 1 percent of men don't qualify. The court ruled that height and weight cannot be used as job qualifiers, so some systems set up physical strength requirements. In New York City in 1978 seventy-nine women took the test to become firefighters. All failed because of the physical strength test. When one of the women filed a discrimination suit, the court ruled in her favor. A test has to predict actual performance on the job. The judge said the test had nothing to do with on-the-job performance.

"Another thing, employers put in job requirements that are not really part of the job to keep women out. They might specify that a particular course or type of experience is required that women applicants wouldn't have."

With a disgusted look on her face, Pam said, "It looks like employers can pretty much keep women out of jobs if they want to."

"That's where the laws and women's organizations have made the big difference. Women have to know their rights and then go after them," Ellen reminded her.

"Oh, that reminds me. I didn't realize that guys making wise comments to women was harassment. You know, the guys do it at school all the time," Pam said. "I guess I never really thought about it."

"Sexual harassment is any kind of unwanted sexual attention on the job," Ellen told Pam. "That includes all the verbal stuff like the comments the boys make in the hall or on the street. Harassment includes being looked at in a sexual way, touching, pinching, patting, brushing up against your body. Supervisors sometimes offer promotions if women go to bed with them. And, of course, the more serious things like assault and rape are included. Lots of times a man will threaten to fire a woman if she won't give in to him. There are all kinds of ways the guy can make the woman suffer on the job if he doesn't get his way."

"Is a lot of that going on?" asked Pam.

"Sure is," Ellen replied. "A lot more than is ever reported. Most of the time the woman quits or asks for a transfer to get out of the situation. Despite laws about it, proving harassment is really hard. Most women don't want to go through the hassle. They're usually embarrassed and humiliated by the man's behavior. They're afraid, too. The men are usually higher-ups who can fire them or make their lives miserable. Most of all, they don't want their families to know what's happening. They think they'll be accused of coming on to the man.

"If they do report it, most male supervisors treat it as a joke. They tell the woman she should expect that when she's working with men. They call her a troublemaker or say she's trying to get even with someone. Women think it won't do any good to report the harassment. It's easier to leave the situation."

"I think that's terrible!" Pam exclaimed. "There should be some way to protect women from that."

"The laws are there," Ellen said. "Going to court is really awful for a woman, though. It's humiliating. The EEOC is trying to enforce the laws. Their guidelines say that employers have to take steps to prevent harassment. They're supposed to let employees know that the company doesn't approve of harassment and that the employees have the right to report it. Court cases have held employers responsible for harassment because they didn't do anything about it.

"One reason women don't report harassment is because they don't know how. Anyone who is sexually harassed can contact the EEOC for information and help in filing a complaint. It takes a lot of courage to file a complaint. More women are, though, because they want jobs and want to get promotions and get ahead. They don't want to be harassed. More important, they don't want to be afraid that the harasser will be able to get back at them for turning him in. It's just slow."

"It's bad enough putting up with the garbage from the boys at school. I hate to think of having it at work," Pam said.

"I think putting up with it at school just encourages them to keep doing it later. I think we ought to try to do something about it now," Ellen said. At Pam's startled look, she said, "I'm not sure what to do, but I'm sure thinking about it. Maybe all of us girls should get together and talk about it."

Pam took a deep breath and slowly exhaled. "That's taking a pretty big step, Ellen. You said it takes courage to file a complaint. I think it'll take courage to do something about the boys' harassment here at school. I'm not sure I can handle that."

"It feels pretty scary to me, too," Ellen confided, "but if we had others to go along with us..."

The girls continued to discuss the idea as they left the Pit Stop and walked home. They agreed to bring up the idea at the meeting on Wednesday. They especially wanted the boys' reactions.

SEX DISCRIMINATION IN THE WORKPLACE

Almost 45 percent of the nation's work force is female. Women have taken 80 percent of the new jobs created since 1980. By the year 2000 women will make up most of the workforce if that trend continues. Unequal pay, limited opportunities for promotion, and other forms of discrimination are important issues for young women who will soon be part of the that workforce.

Job discrimination can start even before you leave

school, as Pam and Ellen discovered. You may be counseled away from classes that give the background for
technical jobs. If you're thinking in stereotypes, you may
not be considering occupations that have traditionally been
filled by men. Good career guidance in high school opens
your mind to all available options.

One researcher says that equal pay for equal work is
pretty much a reality. The 10 to 20 percent wage gap
between men and women is the result of discrimination.
Discrimination in wages is mainly due to job segregation.
Women are detoured into jobs that have always had low
wages—such as clerical jobs—or they choose the more
traditional jobs because of their own stereotypic thinking.
Men don't want those jobs because of the low pay. However, until men enter a field it will remain underpaid. Just
as women's entering a field brings wages down, consider-
able numbers of men entering a field raises the wages.
Many researchers believe that job segregation will continue until men enter fields traditionally held by women.

A man entering an occupation that is traditionally female
is often a victim of discrimination. Verbal harassment from
other men and from women, too, is common. As usual, the
question of manhood comes up. Most harassment implies
that he's less than a man for doing "women's work." Male
dancers and artists are often accused of being homosexual.
Male secretaries are unusual, and people make jokes about
them and question their masculinity. Whether female or
male, choosing a job that is traditionally for the other sex
sets you up for hassles.

Another area of discrimination is job promotion. Ellen
told Pam of the bias against female supervisors. Male
executives feel uncomfortable with women on the same
level. Women who are promoted to high positions sense

that they're considered outsiders and even intruders by their male associates.

Women executives work long hours and often sacrific their homelife to get ahead. They're judged differently from male executives in little ways that seem like nothing until they're added together. If a woman speaks with a questioning tone, she's thought to lack confidence. If she smiles too much, she may not get the promotions that a smiling man gets. If she's willing to listen to people who work under her, it may be taken as a sign of weakness. She is always on inspection, with people looking for things to criticize. Some women told researchers that they don't get the authority that goes with their position unless they learn to act like a man. If they do become more aggressive and manlike, they may lose the special qualities they bring to the job as a woman.

Studies show that male supervisors discriminate against females when making decisions about promotions and training. Females with the same qualifications as males are less likely to be promoted. They're also less likely to be chosen to go to training conferences. When women make decisions, supervisors are less likely to support them but will support the same decisions made by men. Also, women who are capable and skilled are often disliked because of their ability. Sex-role stereotyping results in women and their work being undervalued at every level, from lowest to highest.

Jobs are considered nontraditional when less than 25 percent of those employed are of either sex. Women have made progress in many professional fields. By 1987 over 25 percent of those in managerial positions were women. However, less than 20 percent of physicians, lawyers, and judges were female. Under 10 percent of dentists, firefighters, and engineers were women. Only 12.6 percent of architects and 11.4 percent of police and detectives were female. Construction, heavy equipment operations, mechanics and repair, forestry and fishing, all have very low percentages of women workers.

Although women are making progress getting into some of the male-dominated fields, men are making little effort to break into traditionally female fields. Over 95 percent of registered nurses, practical nurses, receptionists, secretaries, child-care workers, dental assistants, and teacher's aides are female. Men have made little effort to get into clerical positions other than computer operations or supervision. As Ellen learned, job segregation and discrimination keep women in low-paying jobs.

SEXUAL HARASSMENT

In a nationwide survey taken by a leading magazine, nine thousand clerical and professional women were questioned about sexual harassment. Ninety-two percent reported "unpleasant and annoying behavior" by male workers. At Arizona State University 1,500 faculty, students, and staff were interviewed. Thirteen percent of the women and 5 percent of the men said they had been sexually harassed. In a study of working women in New York, 70 percent said they had been sexually harassed. Fifty-two percent believed nothing would be done about it. Forty-two percent thought they would be humiliated and 30 percent were afraid of being blamed if they reported it.

Sexual harassment, as Ellen explained, is any unwanted sexual attention on the job. It includes comments about her body made to the teenage girl filling orders by the teenage boy wrapping hamburgers. When the boss comes by and puts his arm around you and you don't want it there, it's a form of harassment. The Equal Employment Opportunity Commission gives the following definition of sexual harassment.

Unwelcome sexual advances, requests for sexual favors and other verbal or physical conduct of a sexist nature constitute sexual harassment when

(1) submission to such conduct is made either explicitly or implicitly a term or condition of an individual's employment; [That means the person being harassed must agree to do what the harasser wants or allow the offensive behavior to continue to keep a job or to be hired in the first place.]

(2) submission to or rejection of such conduct by an individual is used as the basis for employment decisions affecting such individual; [It is harassment if the person must submit to get a promotion or other considerations on the job, or if he or she refuses it means no promotion and getting the "dirty jobs."] or

(3) such conduct has the purpose or effect of unreasonably interfering with an individual's work performance or creating an intimidating, hostile, or offensive working environment. [Harassment occurs if the person feels afraid of the person doing the harassing, feels anger and antagonism from the harasser, or is offended by the behavior.]

The victims of harassment are usually women. Men have been harassed, but it isn't common. Women seldom harass male coworkers. When women don't cooperate with their harasser, they are often punished. They don't get promotions or normal advancement is slowed down or stopped. They are transferred against their wishes or fired. Their job responsibilities may be taken away. They're given tasks that are insulting to their ability or jobs that no one wants to do. Many quit or ask for transfer to get away from the harassment.

Sexual harassment is a form of discrimination. Title VII of the Civil Rights Act of 1964 prohibits employment discrimination on the basis of race, color, religion, national origin, or sex. Sexual harassment is unlawful because it causes different treatment of workers based on sex.

Ellen was right when she said that employers must take steps to prevent harassment. The EEOC suggests that employers raise the subject of harassment and express their disapproval. It's also recommended that employers develop a system for carrying out the law, including telling employees of their right to file claims. Employers are urged to develop ways to make everyone aware of the problem.

If harassment is reported and the employer does nothing about it, he or she can be held responsible. Successful court cases have caused employers all over the country to take harassment more seriously.

In 1980 a student at Yale University filed a sexual harassment charge against a professor under Title IX. She claimed that the professor offered her an A in exchange for certain sexual favors. She won the case when the court ruled that "academic advancement conditioned upon submission to sexual demands constitutes sex discrimination in education."

Although there are no laws concerning one student's sexually harassing another at school, Title IX of the Education Act is being looked at closely. Some people think that sexual harassment of students is a form of discrimination and is covered. However, Title IX has to do only with specific school programs or activities that are federally funded. The student would have to be involved in a program or activity that gets money directly from the government before the harassment would be covered.

Laws are already in place in protect students from sexual harassment by teachers. If a teacher is in any way sexual toward a student, he or she should be reported immediately.

It's hard to say under what conditions one student's harassing another would come under the law, if at all. Under ordinary circumstances student harassment in a classroom should be reported to the teacher and the principal.

The kind of harassment Pam referred to could be confronted in several ways. Talk to other girls who have experienced the harassment, and ask for their cooperation. As a group the girls could assertively tell the boys that they don't appreciate the comments and want them to stop. Such a confrontation might go like this:

Girls: We want you to know that we feel insulted when comments are made about our bodies or our clothes. We don't like to be called "babes" either. We want you to stop doing that.

Boys: Hey, man, we didn't mean anything by it. We were just foolin' around.

Girls: We want you to stop.

The boys may laugh or get angry or have some other reaction. Ignore that for the moment. If you need to say something, simply repeat, "We want you to stop." If the harassment continues after you've talked to the boys, report it to the principal and ask her or him to do something about it.

You could report the offensive behavior to the principal or administrator in charge of discipline without confronting the boys yourself. Be sure to take a written report of the exact harassment that is going on.

Another approach might be to work through a counselor or teacher. Have the adult call the boys to the office and you confront them in the presence of the adult. That would give you a chance to express your feelings in a safe place. It would also provide an opportunity for discussion if the boys need to talk about the behavior and their feelings about your reactions. Explaining your feelings about being sexually harassed gives the boys a different way of looking at their behavior. Consequently, they're more likely to stop the behavior.

Neither Pam nor Ellen wanted to confront the boys at school by themselves. They needed the support of other young women. The support is in your school and community. You can join with others to confront the issue of sexual harassment.

CHAPTER 7

Sexism and
the Media

During lunch Alex Richards looked for Gina Augustino. He found her sitting on the lawn with Chris Hollis. "I'm glad I found you two," Alex said.

"What's up?" asked Gina.

"I want to check out some things about the sexism project with you. You know, I'm working on sexism in the media." The girls nodded. "Well, I want your opinion on some things."

Both girls said they'd be happy to help, so Alex went on. "When I hear media, I think of television, radio, and newspapers, so that's where I started. After we talked yesterday, Chris, I was more aware of sex roles and sexism in general. It made me look at things a little differently. When I got home my mother was watching a game show on TV. I realized that game show hosts are men, and most of the contestants are women. The women on some of the shows are all excited and breathless and squeal all the time—like on 'The Price Is Right.' You know, just like a woman."

"I think that's a pretty fair description," agreed Chris. "Shows like 'Love Connection' are really sexist to both men and women."

"Oh, yeah!" exclaimed Gina. "I remember when 'The Newlyweds' was followed by 'Divorce Court.' Mom used to say it was great programming: After they got through on the 'Newlyweds' they were ready for the divorce court. Those shows were really sexist."

"Soap operas are sexist, too," Chris said. "I love 'em, but Mom pointed out how sexist they are, and she's right. The women's lives are centered around men whether or not the women have a job. Their jobs are usually stereotypic, too. They're nurses or work in offices. Most of the men are professionals. You don't see many carpenters, plumbers, or telephone linemen as leading men. They're not as desirable to women, and it's women who watch the soaps. So there's some male sexism, too."

"They always have a woman who's after someone else's man and makes trouble," Gina offered. "That's a stereotype, too."

"They portray every female sex role you can think of," Chris added.

"The advertising is sure aimed at women," Alex commented. "The big advertisers sell soap. That's why they're called soap operas. Anyway, Procter and Gamble, General Foods, Colgate-Palmolive, Coca-Cola, and Lever Brothers are the major advertisers. Three of the five sell soap and one other sells soap pads. They all depend on women to buy their products."

"You know what else," Gina added. "Procter and Gamble sells a bunch of different detergents, and they don't care which one you buy. General Foods doesn't care if you buy

Yuban, Maxwell House, Maxim, or Sanka coffee. They make them all, also choose any one you want."

"Women appear in almost all the commercials for those products, too," Alex reminded her. "Men are in some of the ads, but they don't use the cleansers or whatever. They just talk about them, but women use them. I read about a study done by Joanne Cantor, and Daniel Bretl, two psychologists from the University of Wisconsin. They analyzed almost 400 television ads. They found that women still far outnumber the men in parenting roles and in ads for household goods. They also found that more than 90 percent of the narrators are male even though research shows that female voices are just as effective."

"I saw that article when I was looking for sex-role stuff." Gina caught her bottom lip in her teeth while she thought. "Didn't that same article say that there are more teenage girls on TV than boys?" she asked.

"Yeah," Alex said. "The article talked about that report by the National Commission on Working Women. It said that girls' characters were 'more passive and less individualized' and that looks were more important than brains. It said that plots were about clothes and boys, and intelligent girls were even social misfits in some of the shows. Do you agree with that?" Alex wanted to know.

The girls looked at each other and named some shows with teenage female characters. They looked thoughtful, talked about it a bit, and nodded their heads. "Yep, I have to agree," Chris said.

"Me, too," came from Gina. "TV isn't a total sexist wasteland, though. Some shows have good female characters. Even *MS* magazine likes "China Beach," "Heart-Beat," and "Kate and Allie." There've been some good specials too."

"Not many, though," Chris put in. "There are more

sexist than nonsexist roles, especially on prime-time TV."

"What about the news?" Alex asked.

"What about it?" Gina retorted.

"Well, there are lots of women reporters and anchors. Most local stations have a female anchor. The major networks have lots of female reporters. Women have pretty well established themselves in the news media," Alex retorted.

"Yeah, and what do they talk about?" Chris broke in.

"Well, the news," was Alex's answer.

"And who's the news about? Men, that's who," she informed him. "Most of the news stories have to do with men. President Bush did this, Senator Somebody (and there are only a couple of women in the Senate) did that. Males dominate sports reports, and most sports reporters are men. And there are more stories about male sports than female. Foreign leaders are usually men. Wars involve men. Pro-life and pro-choice confrontation involves more women than men, but it's mainly men in government who are voting for or against changes in abortion laws. You have to admit that more news involves men than women," Chris concluded.

"Well, then, that must be true in the newspapers too," Alex remarked. "But there are a lot of women reporters, too. And what used to be called the women's section or society section of the paper has more in it than wedding announcements and who gave what party. There are columns besides child care and 'Dear Abby,' too," he said.

"Hey, you must be reading the 'Scene' section of the paper," Gina gave Alex a playful punch. "Good for you. You're right, there's lots more in it."

"There are the usual happy homemaker and how-to-be-a-good-mommy things too. There's nothing wrong with that as long as it's balanced with the other," Chris reminded them. My mother says that putting everything regarding women in one section of the paper is as sexist as not including it. She says articles about women's issues are newsworthy enough to be in the news section."

They discussed Chris's point, and then Alex said, "Another thing I wanted to ask you about is magazines. I looked at some at the supermarket the other day. There's sure a lot, but they're pretty much the same. I particularly looked at the ones for teenage girls. They're full of advertisements for makeup and clothes. Most of the articles are about dating and boys."

"Most of the women's magazines are like that, too. There are some that don't promote the sex-role stereotypes, but even those put a lot of focus on female-male relationships. That's an important topic to almost everyone," Chris said seriously. "I think the ads for cosmetics and clothes are okay as long as the magazine is balanced. I keep coming back to that. There's nothing wrong with wanting to look good and liking clothes. It's when that keeps you stuck in a stereotype that it's not good."

"Most of the magazines I looked at weren't balanced at all," Alex said. "I think they're pretty much aimed at particular audiences, too. Some are for married women who are interested in home and children type things. Others are for younger women who are interested in clothes and makeup and glamour. They could be married, but most would be single. There's lots of how-to-get-a-man stuff and how to keep a man. At least, that's the way it looked to me," Alex confided.

"I think it's because the magazines look at women as consumers and not thinkers," Chris said. "Advertising in general does that, and magazines need advertisers to survive."

"I want to make another point about advertising," Alex

said. "Lots of times women are used in commercials and magazine advertising just to add sex to it. They're used as sex objects just to sell products."

"Speaking of sex objects, what do you think about songs?" asked Chris.

"I haven't thought about it," Alex admitted.

"Knowing about sexist stereotyping ruined some of my favorite songs for me," said Gina.

"Why's that?" Alex asked her.

"Well, they're all about how you're everything to me or let me be everything to you. The guy is always the big strong man and he's going to make everything right for her. Or else she's sad because he left and she can't live without him. Of course, if a guy sings it, he can't live without her. Then there are all the 'You done me wrong' songs. You know the stuff."

"Yeah, I know what you mean," Alex assured her. "I'm not sure I know what you mean about sex objects, Chris."

"Well, a lot of the songs talk about sex. I think maybe it's the videos as much as the words that show females as sex objects," Chris explained.

"Music videos exploit sex, I think," said Alex. "I didn't think much about it until I started working on this project. Besides the sexist stereotyping, there's a lot of sexually suggestive stuff in videos. I agree with you, Chris, now that you point it out. Heavy metal bands are the worst offenders."

"It's not just that sex is exploited," Chris said. "It's the way females are exploited sexually. They're dressed in tight clothes. They move their bodies sexually. When they're with guys, the way the guy touches them is sexual. Mom says it's no wonder kids get sexually involved really young."

"I think the songs tell you you're supposed to have sex, especially if you love each other," Gina remarked. "I think they really encourage it. They make you feel like everybody's doing it, and there's something wrong with you if you don't."

"That's all over TV and movies, too," Chris declared.

"That reminds me," Alex said. "Sex-role stereotyping in movies is still the rule rather than the exception. Women are getting stronger parts that show them as independent, with minds of their own. They stand up for their rights and aren't portrayed stereotypically. But a lot more movies keep the stereotypes. The ones made especially for teenagers are probably the worst."

"You mean like the horror movies where the girls scream and cringe and cry and hang on to the guys?" When Alex assured her those were the ones, Gina continued, "They're really sexist, I think. The girls are always the victims. They guys are either brutes or they rescue the girls."

"If two people are left alive, though, it's usually the villain and one of the females, and she always wins in the end. Isn't that kind of like females are better?" Alex wondered.

"I think it's more like good wins over bad. Like "Star Wars." The good guys always win," Chris said.

"I suppose you're right," Alex agreed. "I hadn't thought of it that way. I guess that's what makes "Rambo" so popular, too."

"Oh, man, you talk about a sex-role stereotype, you just named the worst kind," Chris roared. "If Rambo isn't macho to the max, I don't know what is."

"That's one of the most popular roles. There's the strong, silent type," Gina chimed in.

"There's the Burt Reynolds funny-but-tough guy who

has a heart of gold and outsmarts the bad guys all the time. He's always just a little bad himself, but not a total outlaw," Alex offered.

"Yeah, and he always has a female he has to take care of," reminded Gina.

"You have tough loners who go against the evil in the world, and the James Bonds who are super spies and have beautiful girls all over the world waiting to hop in bed with them," Chris added.

"Don't forget the men who suffer at the hands of evil women," Alex prompted. The three talked about men's roles for a minute, and then Alex mentioned some typical roles for women. "You know, there's the sexpot, the dumb airhead everybody loves, the bitch, the goody-goody..."

"The super mom, the good-natured grandmother, the long-suffering wife, the intellectual who only needs a man to come down to earth, the tough businesswoman who finds real happiness when a child comes into her life..." Both girls thought of the roles of women in movies. They named movies and then gave a name to the stereotyped roles that were played.

"You know what," Chris said, "my mom's favorite TV show is really loaded with stereotypes. She loves "Golden Girls." There's the sexpot, the lovable airhead, the tough-as-nails-with-a-heart-of-gold, and an old lady who can say outrageous things because of her age. The storylines aren't sexist, but the characters are sure stereotypes."

"I guess that proves that sex-role stereotypes get into everything," Gina observed.

"You can enjoy the shows even though you're aware of the sexism," Chris said. "Like Mom likes *Golden Girls* and I like soap operas."

"I don't think you can totally eliminate sexism." Chris

looked thoughtful as she reflected on what Alex had just said.

"You know, Alex, I don't know if it's important that there be no sexism at all."

Gina and Alex were surprised to hear that from Chris. Alex teasingly warned her not to say that where a female activist could hear her. Then he seriously asked her to explain what she meant.

"Well," Chris said slowly, "women and men are different. Sexism goes back to the beginning of time. It's unrealistic to expect it to be totally abolished—at least, not for a long time. I think what's possible is that we can become more aware and do what we can to stop the progression of it. I think we can make the world less sexist for our children...and I guess we have an obligation to do that. If the eight of us on this project are affected enough to make some changes in our lives, we'll have an effect on lots of other people."

"I think I know what you're saying, Chris. Each one of us comes in contact with a lot of people just doing what we do and going where we go. If we are less sexist ourselves, others will notice it and maybe we'll influence them to change, too. Isn't that it?" Alex asked.

"Besides that, we can talk about sexist stuff when it happens. We girls have been talking about letting the guys know that we don't like their comments about us when we walk by them in the hall," Gina told Alex.

"We can do a lot of things. If we think about it, I'll bet we can do some things to have an influence on the media, too," Chris said.

"I think I'll think about that, and maybe I can have some suggestions for the group at the meeting Wednesday." With that final thought from Alex, the bell rang for the end of lunch, and the three young people went in for afternoon classes.

MEDIA AND SEXISM

The media play an important part in your life. Mass media entertain, inform, persuade you and influence your opinions and attitudes. You're repeatedly bombarded with messages of how men and women behave. The dominant message is that women should be feminine and men should be masculine.

As Alex, Gina, and Chris noticed, commercials are perhaps the worst offenders. If you believe the commercials, women stay at home, are allowed out of the house only in the company of men, and are rarely allowed to drive cars. They have constant aches and pains that require taking a variety of medications, or they're busily seeing that their husbands and children are receiving the medications they need for their various ailments. A major interest of women in commercials is to look more beautiful or smell better. They live their lives waiting on others or improving themselves so that others will be happier. In a study of 1,241 commercials made by the New York chapter of the National Organization of Women, only 0.3 percent (3 in 1,000) portrayed women as living independent lives.

Female dependence is also promoted in the television shows that come between the commercials. Women are most often shown in narrow, traditional roles. A few programs show women as competent, capable, and assertive. In most of the highly rated shows, however, women are not really part of the action. They add the "sugar and spice" or the sex interest for the male characters. If they have a central role, they're often powerful women who gained their power through evil manipulations.

The typical sex roles are still found in most movies, also, as Chris, Gina, and Alex pointed out. Movie ratings evaluate sex in movies, not sexism. Some of the old G-rated movies are the most sexist. Children's movies show women and men in traditional sex roles. Mothers take care of the house and family. Fathers go out and earn a living to support the family. If the father has to leave for any reason, the oldest son is told that he's the man of the family and in charge—even if he has an older sister. Girls learn to be like Mother. They are shown as dependent on males. If they are teenaged, their boyfriends are their protectors.

As Alex said, women have established themselves in the news media. It was a long and difficult struggle. One example of that struggle occurred in Washington, D.C. Women reporters were not allowed in the National Press Club. When important people make speeches in Washington, they most often speak at the Press Club. Women reporters had to sit in the visitors' gallery of the men-only club and couldn't ask questions of the speakers. It took from 1954 to 1971 for women to be admitted to the National Press Club. Newswomen all over the United States have worked hard to get where they are.

Having female reporters on a newspaper doesn't guarantee that the paper will be nonsexist. Story assignments are generally made by men, and if they don't think a story is important it isn't covered. Also, the positioning of the story in the paper determines how many people will read it. When women's issues are found only in the women's section, they've been committed to a sexist burial.

Important women's issues are often reported with a sexist slant. It's not unusual for a headline to report something like "Five Women Quit State Highway Patrol Academy." Buried somewhere in the story might be the fact that twenty-seven men quit during the training also. When women unite and march for a cause, the picture with the story may show the forcible removal of twelve who disregarded police requests to stay in one particular area. After sensationalizing that part of the story, the piece will go on to say that 2,500 women walked in an orderly way and made their protest known to the governor. The people who skim the paper come away with the idea that those who demonstrate for women's rights are militant, disobedient, and disorderly.

As Chris pointed out, men dominate in the news and sports. Once in a while the women's section may run a picture of a bride and groom; never do you see just a picture of the groom. Under a photograph in *Newsweek* before the 1988 election was the caption, "George Bush and Dan Quayle (and their wives)." Women are given their identification through their husbands.

What is seen and read has a great influence on the development of beliefs about sex roles. The magazines that are in the house are looked at by children before they can read. They learn what society expects of them from the messages sent through pictures. News magazines and general-interest magazines judge women athletes through sexist lenses. They acknowledge their accomplishments and add sexist comments such as this one from *Time*: "Little Szabo looks like she would sooner fall off the balance beam than neglect her eye shadow."

The *Sports Illustrated* annual swimsuit edition has long been objected to by women as a notorious example of treating women as sex objects. Men's magazines such as *Playboy* not only objectify women but also victimize them. Chris and Alex mentioned this kind of treatment of females in advertising, but men's magazines take it to extremes. Alex reminded Chris that *Playgirl*, *Stud*, and *Hunk* do the same thing to males.

Songs promote sexism by putting women in submissive roles. "You were born to be my baby and I was made to be your man." He's a man, but she's his baby. Sexual victimization is in lyrics like "I'll send you a love letter / Straight from the bottom of my heart / You'll be f___ forever / The candy-coated clown's done his part / I'm your man I'm what you need..."

When songs are on video, the sexuality is even more vivid. The message, as Gina noted, is that sex is not only okay, it's what you want and what you need. If you want it and need it, then you should be doing it. You didn't start getting that message at age sixteen. You got it when you were six or eight or maybe younger if you had older brothers and sisters. Discussions of sexuality, emotional relationships between females and males, the pros and cons of early sex, or even the physical and social consequences of sex are not usually discussed with youngsters. Sex usually "happens" rather than being a mature decision between two people who value, respect, love, and admire each other. With so much flagrant sexuality in all the media, it's difficult for young people to grow up with healthy attitudes and values about sex.

Even though sexism twists and twines its way throughout all parts of our society, it can be cut back, its growth stopped, and some of it uprooted if it isn't nurtured and fertilized and encouraged to grow. You can be a part of preventing further growth of sexism. You do have power to influence the media.

WHAT YOU CAN DO

Two shows that portrayed women in nonsexist ways stayed on the air when viewers objected to their removal. When it was announced that "Cagney and Lacey" would be taken off the air, angry viewers wrote letters, and the show went on for a few more years. Protesting viewers kept "Kate and Allie" on the air a few years later.

If you find a show's sexism to be offensive, write a letter and send copies to your local station, the network, the National Association of Broadcasters, the sponsors of the show or maker of the product you object to, and even the Federal Communications Commission. Your objection won't get the show taken off the air, but it might cause someone to think a moment about the sexism you object to. This is especially true of commercials.

When you write, be sure to give the call letters of the station on which you saw the offensive material, the time and date, exactly what you object to, and what you would like to see instead. If you intend to stop buying a product or watching a show or station, be sure to state that.

If you feel strongly about an ad in a magazine, write the editor of the magazine as well as the company running the ad. Saying that you, as one person, won't buy the magazine or the product may seem like little to worry a company. One little girl wrote a letter to Lionel trains saying that girls like trains, too. The makers of Lionel trains called a press conference and started a new ad campaign starring the little girl.

If you're unhappy with something in a local newspaper or TV program, call the management of the paper or station and talk to them personally. You'd be surprised at how accessible those people are. If you feel very strongly, you can organize a campaign to write letters, make phone calls, or march in front of the building.

Go to your local women's organizations and ask their advice on what to do about media messages—TV, film, magazines, radio—that you find objectionable. Seek support from others. It's especially important to use adult sources because they've had experience in what you want to do.

If there are younger children in your family, talk to them about what they see on TV and in films. Ask their opinions. Help them write letters to express their objections to product advertising. Help girls to explore options beyond the ones shown in sexist programs. Talk about the advertising on children's programs. Spend time talking about stereotypes and help children understand that they have other options.

Awareness of sexism in the media needn't ruin your enjoyment. You can be like Chris and enjoy the soaps yet be aware of the sexism. You may find that you become more selective about what you watch or buy. When something is offensive, take action of some kind. As Alex pointed out, there's a ripple effect to anything you do.

CHAPTER 8

Sexism at Play

As she came around the corner of the building, Gina Augustino nearly bumped into Colleen Madigan, "Oh, hi, Colleen, are you ready for the meeting tomorrow?" Gina asked.

"Yeah, pretty much, thanks to you," Colleen replied. At Gina's questioning look, Colleen went on. "Sunday at the Pit Stop you said some things that made me think a little more about my part in sports and games. You said how little kids want to do the right things that girls or boys are supposed to do. You mentioned how toys reinforce sex roles, and it got me to thinking. I mentioned it to my mother. She found a Sears toy catalog for 1989. She teaches preschool, you know, and she had a school supply catalog that had toys in it, too."

"What did you want them for?" Gina asked.

"I wanted to see if the way the toys are displayed and advertised reinforce the sex-role stereotypes. My mother also dug out an article from a magazine that she had saved. It was written in 1972, and it talked about sexism and toys. It really helped me know what to look for. I thought that in seventeen years things must really have changed, but the stereotypes were as strong as ever. There are some sex-neutral toys like blocks, climbing equipment, and swing sets and some craft sets that picture both boys and girls. 'Tinkertoys' and 'Leggos' have girls and boys on the boxes, but the Sears catalog pictures only boys playing with them. Only boys were pictured with the electronic games and computerized equipment, and only male cartoon characters were pictured on the page of video games.

"There's a little girl looking through the kids' telescope, but boys were looking through the real microscope and telescope. The school supply catalog had a microscope, telescope, periscope, bug box, and kaleidoscope. Only one had an age on it, the periscope for children four to eight, and that's the one the girl was using."

"That's really sexist!" Gina exclaimed.

"That's only the beginning," Colleen said. "The 'Little Homemaker' pages are something else. There are fifteen pictures of children. Boys are in five of them. In three they're eating. In one the boy is just kneeling beside the kitchen set. In the fifth the smiling boy, wearing a padded glove, is standing by an oven with a pie in it, while a girl with an apron on (Guess who made the pie?) leans on the other end of the kitchen set. Even though there are boys in the pictures, they don't cross the sex-role lines at all.

"Of course, there were pages of Barbies and fashion dolls. Barbie and her friends, including the guys, had outfits and accessories. Naturally, Barbie had a pink Corvette and a pink jeep for the beach. You know what really got me? They even had horses called FashionStar Fillies with long manes and tails to style. They come with a hairbrush and accessories—you know, jewelry for their manes and tails."

"That's taking glamour a little far," Gina agreed. "You seem to be extra interested in this. How come?"

"I think it's because I was so unaware of it," Colleen

said. "I knew how sexist sports can be because I had to fight so hard to play soccer with the boys, and even in elementary school there were times when teachers didn't want to let me play with the boys."

"I didn't realize there was so much sexism about toys," Colleen went on. "It was when you mentioned that toys reinforced sex roles that I really began to think about it. You see, we had all kinds of toys in our family. My brother and sister and I all played with the same toys. Andy didn't play with Barbies, but he played with the rag dolls and baby dolls when he was little. Now that I think about it, he played with them until he went to school. I'll bet somebody told him dolls were for girls. Eileen and I always played with the trucks, and the electric train was for everybody. Mom had as much fun with it as we did. We still set it up every year by the Christmas tree."

"My brothers have a train, but I could never play with it," Gina confided in a mournful voice. "If I got near it, they'd yell to my father, and he'd tell me that the train was for the boys. I could watch it, but I couldn't touch it."

"You know, Gina, that's what it said in an article I read. Boys are given action toys and are encouraged to play more actively. The article also talked about the games kids play and the kind of toys they play with. It said that play helps kids cope with disturbing things and lets them practice how to handle situations. If they're mad about something, they can have a doll break something or say something they're not supposed to, and then they scold the doll because they don't want to feel guilty. They can take out aggression crashing cars or building things out of blocks and knocking them down."

"Did you ever have imaginary friends?" Colleen wanted to know. Gina looked a little embarrassed as she nodded. "Well, kids who have imaginary friends are more creative and original because they make up wild stories and do all kinds of things with their imaginary friends."

"Yeah? I've never told anybody about the imaginary friend I had when I was little. I always thought it was kind of stupid and didn't want anybody to know. I don't feel so bad about her now," Gina said.

"This article talked about dramatic play, you know, like when we used to play 'Let's Pretend.' Do you remember doing that?" Colleen asked.

"Oh, sure. We'd set up a whole scene and then say 'Let's pretend you say . . .' and then I'll say, . . .' And then we'd argue because we didn't want to pretend to say what the other person wanted us to pretend to say." As Gina talked, Colleen joined in, and soon both girls were laughing.

"That's supposed to be good for kids to do," Colleen said. "Oh, and remember you were telling me about the difference between boys' and girls' skills in spatial relationships? Well, playing with blocks, climbing, riding, and playing with cars and trains and transportation toys are supposed to build that skill. Those are the things that girls don't do as much as boys. The article said that may be partly why boys have superior skills in visual-spatial relationships later on."

"That sounds reasonable to me," Gina agreed. "You really found out a lot."

"I found out one other thing that makes me feel really good. Women who were 'tomboys' are the most successful and high-achieving in many fields. Female high school athletes have higher grade point averages and set higher goals for themselves than other girls in their classes."

"So we should all go out for sports to raise our grade averages and be more successful," Gina said.

"I don't think that's what the author was saying. But there are some real lifetime benefits from sports. A lot of sports become lifelong recreation. You get pleasure, health benefits, fitness, and you have fun. When you do well, your self-esteem goes up. Sports give you a way to socialize. You learn a lot, too. You learn to understand rules and follow and respect them. You learn to work with others toward a common goal. You even get a chance for leadership. There are all kinds of ways that sports can carry over into your adult life. Even if you're not playing, you can always be a fan. You can coach recreationally. You can play with your kids and the kids in the neighborhood."

"There are lots of sports besides team sports that you can participate in," Gina said. "There's skiing, tennis, skating, dancing, bowling, golf, jogging, swimming. . ."

"Skydiving, hang gliding, surfing, windsurfing, sailing, bicycling, car racing, fishing, kayaking, white water rafting," Colleen chimed in. "And females can do all of them. That's a point I want to make with the group. All the things you named, Gina, are considered to be within the sex role of women. All the things I named are stereotyped as men's sports. That kind of thing limits women. We have to open up our thinking.

"The whole 'weaker sex' thing keeps women from doing lots of fun things. Women don't break any easier than men do. When I first started playing soccer with the team, the boys who hadn't played with me before didn't know how to treat me on the field. Well, they found out if they got in my way I did my best to get them out of my way. They decided they'd better play as rough with me as I did with them. Once we got that taken care of, we got along fine."

"You say we have to open up our thinking. How? And if my thinking is opened up, what do I do about it, and how do I let other women know about it?" Gina's forehead was wrinkled and her expression was intent as if she were challenging Colleen.

"It's not just women who need to realize these things, Gina. Men do, too. We need men who take their daughters fishing and buy them electric trains. Boys need fathers who encourage them to take dancing lessons if that's what they want to do. I'm really lucky because my parents encouraged us to do whatever we wanted to do. I played jacks and jump rope with the girls and football and marbles with the boys. My dad and mom took us all fishing. Mom showed me how to cut bait. She taught me to embroider, and she taught my brother to embroider, too. Dad taught us all how to pass a football. I'm going to be sure that my kids have the same advantage I did."

"You're really lucky, Colleen. There are lots of things I just crossed off and forgot because I'm a girl."

Colleen could see that Gina felt sad about what she had missed, and she asked what had been crossed off her list. "Well, fishing for one thing," Gina admitted.

"Fishing! You can put that one back on your list. You can go fishing with us. Mom'll be excited about having someone to teach how to cut bait!"

Gina protested that she wasn't trying to get an invitation, but Colleen insisted that Gina come home with her right then and get the trip set up. As she hurried off with Colleen, the thought ran through Gina's head that she'd never dreamed a class project would lead to going fishing. The thought of playing with the train at Christmas flashed through her mind as Colleen told about catching her first fish.

THE SERIOUS WORK OF PLAY

Play is the work of children. Through play they develop their bodies and minds. Specific kinds of play develop specific muscles and coordination skills. Manipulative toys

like puzzles, Tinkertoys, Lincoln Logs, and toys that inter-
lock and stack help build hand-eye coordination. Pounding
toys and those that have different shapes to fit into the
right places develop those smaller motor skills, too. Large
muscles and visual-spatial development are promoted by
riding, climbing, block building, and transportation toys.

All children deserve the opportunity to handle, move,
and enjoy those toys. Children learn to create, manipulate,
fantasize, dramatize, analyze, assemble, dismantle, calcu-
late, reason, express, count, cooperate, share, plan, win,
lose, and just have fun through toys. Children play 10,000
hours before they go to first grade. Their personality,
physical well-being, and character are developed by the
toys and games that are their "business" of play.

Toys have no gender. They're nonsexist in and of themselves. The way they are presented to children creates the
sex assigned to toys. Children need only go into toy stores
to know which toys are for girls and which for boys. The
packaging shows them that fathers and sons guide remote-
control cars. You never see a boy on a tea-set box, and the
mop and broom package shows a girl enjoying the thrills of
housekeeping.

Manufacturers, retailers, and advertisers put the toys
out, but it's the adult who puts the toy in the child's life.
Young adults decide for children also. The toys you give
children make a statement and have an influence on them.
To present toys in a nonsexist way, your behavior must be
nonsexist as well. If children are to be willing to cross the
gender lines, they must see adults who practice flexible
roles. Children need models if they are to learn new
behavior.

Toys and other "props" stimulate children to dramatic
play, which is very important in children's emotional and
creative development. Too often sex-role stereotypes stifle

children by the restrictions they impose. In the school-supply catalog under Imaginative Play were costumes for role-playing. A girl was pictured in a mail carrier's jacket and hat and the catalog listing for the costume was "mailman." For girls dress-ups were long dresses, capes in pink, lavender, and light blue, veils, and hats with bows and flowers. Boys wore hats for train engineer, construction worker, police officer, sailor, and firefighter and, of course, there was a Superman outfit.

Children need to know that women work on jobs that require the yellow construction worker's hat and women are firefighters, police officers, and mail carriers. Girls deserve a chance at the hats so they can pretend to build and rescue and drive a train. Girls can wear the astronaut suit or the magician's cape and pretend to pull rabbits out of hats as effectively as boys. A frustrating stereotype that is persisted in by catalogs, advertisers, manufacturers, re-tailers, and people in general is that nurse equals female and doctor equals male. If that stereotype is ever to be eliminated, children can't be subjected to it over and over.

Play offers children opportunity to work through their problems. Child psychologists use dolls to let children reenact traumatic events. The truth of what happened comes out in the dramatic play of the child. Children can let dolls tell the feelings that they themselves are afraid to express. Through the dolls they can voice their terror, rage, and confusion.

When children play "Let's pretend. . ." they're able to dramatize their relationships with others. They can express what they don't understand, and other children help them. They can work out differences with one another and have "pretend" fights that find resolutions to their problems.

Through dramatic play children practice adult roles. They can be parents, shopkeepers, and taxi drivers. A briefcase turns them into a business executive. If they don't have role models and other encouragements, girls won't be shopkeepers, taxi drivers, or business executives. They'll be the mother who stays home and takes care of the house and babies and has dinner ready when the father comes home with his briefcase. There's nothing wrong with that as long as girls know they have the option of driving the taxi or carrying the briefcase.

Sex-role stereotypes come out strongly in the way children play sports. Girls are taught that it's better not to try too hard to win, and boys learn that winning is all there is. Boys need to be taught that it's okay to lose, and okay to lose to a girl. Girls need to be encouraged to do their best, even if it means beating a boy. Competition between the sexes is not the goal. That idea goes back to the "boys are better than girls" nonsense. The idea is to encourage everyone to realize her or his potential.

Learning the rules of the game and how to be a team member are important lessons that sports teach. The foundation of working cooperatively in business and professional life can be found on the playing field. Girls often miss the important lessons from team play because they've participated only in individualistic activities. It's working toward a common goal using group strategy that matters most often in the business world. Developing leadership qualities and refining interaction skills require being part of a group.

Besides the social and intellectual benefits, sports bring recreation and pleasure. Exercise is part of good health and physical fitness, and the sports and games you participate in today will offer you choices for a lifetime of fun and leisure enjoyment. Play is the serious business of children and becomes the pleasure of adults.

WHAT YOU CAN DO

For Young Children. If you have younger brothers, sisters, nieces, nephews, or other children on your gift lists, be conscious of the toys you give them. When you buy the golf club and ball, consider taking it out of the package with the boy pictured swinging the club before you wrap it. Packaging that sends a sexist message need not be seen by the child who receives your gift.

Instead of the pink Barbie car, give Barbie a less sexist car. Who knows, the child may play with the car for a while instead of with the Barbie.

Encourage a child's creativity and curiosity with gifts. Seeds and a flowerpot or a small plant bring the joy of watching things grow. You may inspire a budding writer with the gift of a notebook and pen for a journal. A "starter" stamp-collecting kit could stimulate a life-long hobby. Assemble a "craft set" for making collages by putting different kinds of beans and lentils in plastic bags. Add some buttons, trims, braids, and sequins in their own plastic bags. Look around for odds and ends that add texture and color. Put your "kit" in a box and include a note encouraging the child to refill the box with treasures of her or his own for future works of art. Use your creativity to bring out the creativity in a child.

If you're around children, watch them and listen to their conversations during play. Be aware of how many sexist stereotypes are part of them already. Intervene in a sensitive way when one four-year-old tells another that she can't be the pilot of the "pretend" plane because girls don't fly airplanes. Tell them that women do fly airplanes and then leave them to their playing.

If you hear "I can't," "I'm afraid," "I don't know how,"

take the opportunity to help the child. Be a "safety" person
and stand by while they try something new. Encourage
them to try while you watch.

For Older Children.   Brothers or sisters just a few years
younger than you can be motivated to explore activities
that they're hesitant to try because of sexist stereotypes.
Tell your sister who likes softball to sign up for the mixed
team at the neighborhood recreation district. Encourage
your brother who's a good skater to take figure skating
lessons. Be a model yourself and take a risk that crosses the
sex barrier.

For Yourself.   List all the sports and recreational activities that you enjoy or you think you might enjoy. Check
the ones that cross gender barriers. If you don't have any,
think of some! You're limiting yourself. Then choose one
activity and decide how and when you will participate in it.

Experience as many different sporting events as possible. Television covers many sports besides baseball,
football, and basketball. There's car racing, surfing, hang
gliding, skydiving, track, tennis, golf, ballooning, soccer,
polo, field hockey, water polo, diving, figure skating,
speed skating, and more. Both sexes participate in all those
sports. Don't be just a watcher, be a participant.

Males often worry that they won't be good enough, so
they quit before they start. If they have difficulty and
don't do well immediately, they don't want to continue.
Young men need to learn to be a beginner. Give yourself
credit for being willing to try something new and stick with
it. Take on the challenge of badminton. It's harder than
you think, but fun. So what if the girls play better than you
to start with. Stop trying to win, and start having fun.

So you want to go skeet shooting, but you're a girl.

Women shoot skeet. Go by the shooting range and check it out. What else have you wanted to do that "girls don't do"? You can do it if you want to. You don't need to be a star. You just need to try.

CHAPTER 9

Males and Sexism

Paul Rodriguez tapped lightly on the doorframe and leaned his head through the door of his counselor's office. Seeing the serious expression on Paul's face, Mr. Garrett invited him to come in.

"What's on your mind, Paul? You look like you're carrying a pretty heavy load."

"I guess I am," Paul admitted. "I'm working on a project for English, and it's got me thinking about some stuff." After explaining the project, Paul said, "My part of the project is how sexism affects males. I figured if sexism affects females, it must affect males, too."

"Does that mean that you feel pressured into certain kinds of behavior to live up to the male sex-role stereotype?" asked Mr. Garrett.

"Yeah, I guess it does," Paul replied. "On Saturday Stan and I talked about the project. We were talking about sex roles and little kids. You know, I remember when I was six I fell down and cut my hand. Man, I saw all that blood, and I was so scared. I was crying and screaming. When my mother was cleaning it up, my father told me to quit being such a crybaby. He said I had to learn to 'take things like a man.' After that, when I got hurt I tried not to cry. I wanted to be like a man. Mr. Garrett, I was only six years old. What's wrong with a six-year-old's crying when he's hurt?"

"Nothing, Paul, and there's nothing wrong with a six-teen-year-old's crying when he's hurt. That goes for emotional hurts as well as physical." Mr. Garrett looked thoughtful for a moment and then asked, "What else did you find out about feelings?"

"I found out that if I follow the stereotype I'm not supposed to have feelings. Well, I'm not supposed to show them anyway."

As they talked, Paul realized that he still had the feelings that were supposed to be feminine, not masculine. He also felt that there was something wrong with him for having those feelings. When Paul was twelve, his dog died. Paul waited until everyone was out of the house before he went to his room, locked the door, and cried. He told Mr. Garrett that he had felt ashamed of himself ever since.

When Mr. Garrett asked if Paul had ever told a girl that he really liked her, Paul said sure. When asked if he had ever told a boy that he really liked him, Paul's answer was negative.

"I know you're good friends with Jerry King. Why haven't you told him that you value his friendship?" Mr. Garrett asked.

"Oh, c'mon, Mr. Garrett. You know why not." Seeing Mr. Garrett's expression, Paul said, "I get it. That's part of the stereotyping. You can't say something like that to another guy because he might think you're...well, you know."

"Homosexual?" With a questioning look, Mr. Garrett drew out the word slowly. At Paul's nod, he continued. "According to the stereotype, if you express soft, tender feelings to another male, it's a sign of femininity. You're less of a man." Mr. Garrett shook his head sadly and said, "That stereotype robs us males of a whole side of our personality and humanity."

"How or why does that happen?" Paul wondered.

Mr. Garrett explained, "It begins in infancy. The most influential person in a baby's life is his mother. For the first five or so years of your life, your mother is everything to you. During that time, you realize that you're a boy, and boys are different from girls. You also realize that you're a separate person from your mother, and you begin the separation from her. Recognizing gender differences and accepting your gender are part of a process. Learning to like and live your gender becomes your job. For boys, living their gender means not doing anything that can be considered feminine.

"To make the separation from mother complete, you can't get too close to any females. Emotional closeness can harm your masculinity. You have to keep yourself separate, prove that you're not a woman."

"But girls don't have to prove they're not men," Paul protested.

"That brings up another point, Paul. Did you and Stan talk about the stereotype that males have to be best?" At Paul's nod, Mr. Garrett continued. "Girls don't have to prove anything, Paul. They don't have to give up their identification with their mother. They don't have to give up emotional closeness.

"When boys identify with fathers and other males, they learn the regulations that come through casual remarks such as your father made to you when you cried. Some rules come as standards: 'Put everything you've got into it and play to win.' Others come as out-and-out threats. My father told me that the next time I came home crying that somebody had hit me, he'd hit me himself. I was to fight back and give as good as I got.

"Boys learn that they must keep their emotional distance and maintain their emotional masculinity. That causes them to exaggerate female weaknesses and those characteristics they see as male strengths. Out of the exaggeration comes the need to be better than the female. You have to be boss to show strength. The avoidance of anything female and exaggeration of anything male are a defensive wall to maintain separation and masculinity. Males must be constantly on guard for signs of weakness, emotionalism, or closeness that might indicate a crack in that wall. If they see a crack, it has to be plastered over with some outward show of masculinity. What we end up with is the stereotype of the strong silent male who can handle anything."

Mr. Garrett could see that Paul was struggling with the rules for being masculine, so he asked him to mention some of the rules that particularly bothered him. They talked about fear; how words like "scaredy-cat," "coward," "wimp," "gutless," and "sissy" drive males to destructive behavior. Paul told of the time he ran across a busy street when he was eight because other boys called him "chicken."

They talked about closeness and touching. Paul said, "Now I understand why boys don't touch each other. We're taught that touching means sex."

"There are ways and times for touching, though," Mr. Garrett reminded him. "Guys walk up and punch each other in the arm or squeeze hands to see who flinches first in a handshake."

"In ball games they grab each other and pound each other on the back," Paul broke in.

"If you notice on TV, they even pat each other on the behind," Mr. Garrett added. "Under those conditions, it's okay, but don't do it to a guy in the hall."

Paul said, "Better not do it to a girl in the hall either." They laughed, then Paul grew serious again. "I've been thinking about what you said about telling Jerry how I feel about his friendship. You know, I wish I could do that, but I'd feel stupid. Do you ever do it with your friends?"

"I've done it with my very best friend. I felt I was taking a big chance when I did it, but I also felt sure that he would understand and appreciate it."

"And what happened?"

"He told me how much I mean to him. Our friendship is more important to us than ever."

"But that kind of thing is unusual, isn't it, Mr. Garrett? I mean, two guys talking like that," Paul suggested.

"You're right, Paul, but we had taken a class together on relationships. He's a counselor, too. Because of class discussions, I was pretty sure where he stood. I had just read a book on assertiveness for young people. You might be interested in it. It's called *Coping Through Assertiveness*. The book recommended making some positive assertions such as telling a friend how much you appreciate the friendship. So I did, and I'm really glad I did. I'm trying to break out of some of the sex-role stereotypes that have kept me in a bind."

Hearing Mr. Garrett talk about feeling tied up by the stereotypes made Paul feel less different. He had thought there was something wrong with him for having the feelings that he did.

"It's not that I can't live up to some of the macho stuff. I don't want to," Paul said. "I like girls all right, but I don't think making it sexually with girls is the main goal of life. I get sick of listening to some of the guys talk about girls. They either talk about who they already made it with or who they'd like to. That's supposed to make you somebody. Well, I'm not like that."

"An interest in girls is natural," Mr. Garrett said. "A lot of the guys are exaggerating their sex triumphs to gain status. It's a way of demonstrating masculinity. It goes back to the concept of having to prove your manhood over and over. Teenage boys realize that sex is considered an important way to prove manhood. That's why all the talk and why so many boys get sexually involved before they're really ready for it. I think recognizing you're not ready for sex is a sign of maturity and true manhood."

"Are you telling me that all the feelings I think make me a freak really don't?" Paul asked.

"You're a human being, Paul, and human beings have feelings. The male sex-role stereotype with its restrictions on feelings robs you of your humanness. The fear of appearing feminine limits you horribly. Emotional expression is labeled feminine. Showing pain, asking for help, touching, being concerned about your health are all considered feminine. There's tremendous pressure to drink to prove you're a man. If you don't drink, you're ridiculed. The constant drive to be better than others, to be the most powerful, the biggest man keeps you from being a whole human being. You have to deny your needs as a person if you live up to the stereotype. The conflict you feel is between your needs as a human being and the sex-role stereotypes you're programmed with. From what I can tell, your needs as a human being are beginning to score more points."

"I'm not sure what's happening right now," Paul confessed. "I know that I gave up trying to be best a long time ago. I've felt as if I let down everybody, including myself. When I don't want to join in the talk about girls and sex, I feel there must be something wrong with me. Because I don't like sports, I feel I let my dad down. When I talked to Stan the other day, I could see something was wrong with my thinking, but I wasn't sure what it was. Now I can see that thinking I had to live up to the stereotype and not making it—and not wanting to—is at least part of what's wrong."

"It depends on how you look at it," Mr. Garrett suggested. "I think not wanting to live up to the stereotypes is a sign of what's right about you. You're becoming aware of your own needs and opinions. So far you haven't had support. You've followed the stereotype and kept your feelings inside. Now that you've had a chance to bring them out and look at them, you can begin to get support for them."

"Where do I get support?"

"Right here. That's what you came in for today, wasn't it?" Mr. Garrett's smile told Paul that he had come to the right place. "I think you'll probably find support in the project group. It sounds as if Stan is doing some thinking too. As you look for support, you'll find it. Most of all, Paul, you'll find it in yourself. As you believe more and more in your own feelings and convictions, you'll find it easier to be who you are. You'll stop worrying about whether or not someone else thinks you're a wimp."

Looking very thoughtful, Paul remarked, "Part of my problem is my own sexism, isn't it? I have to look at my stereotypes about men and women and how sexist I am. I think it all fits together."

"That's right. The degree to which you have to defend your masculinity will pretty much determine your need to keep women 'in their place.' When you see yourself as a human being, you can look at women as human beings. You're already doing that even though you don't realize it," Mr. Garrett said.

"How's that?" The quizzical look on Paul's face made Mr. Garrett smile.

"Your discomfort when the guys talk about making it with girls is partly because you sense the disrespect toward the girls. Am I right?"

"I hadn't thought about it before, but, yeah, that's part of it. You've sure made me think a lot. I'm not as confused as I was. I think I know what I want to tell the group tomorrow. I'm not through thinking about this, though. If you don't mind, I'd like to come back and talk some more in a few days."

Assuring Paul that he was welcome any time, Mr. Garrett put an arm around Paul's shoulders and walked him to the door. As he walked down the hall, Paul realized how good that arm had felt. He also realized how much it meant to him to have a man tell him it was all right for him to feel as he did. He walked out of the building with his shoulders a little straighter and his head a little higher.

LIVING UP TO THE MALE STEREOTYPE

From the time he was a little boy, Paul was bombarded with "Be a man" messages. He couldn't cry when he hurt without feeling he had fallen short of the ideal. When he didn't want to participate in "sexploiting" girls with the other guys at school, he felt there must be something wrong with him. His natural human tendencies were in conflict with the sex-role stereotype that was a part of him. The English project gave him an opportunity to explore the stereotype and how it was affecting him. It gave him a chance to see options where he'd never seen them before. Perhaps he won't give up his humanness for the sake of putting on a manly front.

Even though men have held a position of power in relation to women, they've paid a heavy price for their dominance. To keep women down, men have to work hard to build themselves up. Any sign of weakness means a loss of power and position. Maintaining their superior status becomes a driving force. They couldn't have kept such control without the help of women. Accepting the sex-role stereotypes, women believed themselves to be less than men. They believed it their duty to support men, to follow men, to be subservient to men. The cost to both men and women has been very high.

Women were the first to realize the inequities and how much of themselves they were denying by maintaining the sex-role stereotypes. When women began to work for equal rights, men felt threatened. They thought women wanted to take control, to take over and put them down. They feared the loss of control. The reality underlying the fear is not loss of control but loss of masculinity. According to the stereotype, males are better than females. There's no such thing as equality of the sexes. If males aren't better than females, then females must be better than males. That's frightening to someone who constantly has to prove his manhood.

As Paul found out, males learn early that they must live up to the sex-role stereotype or suffer the ridicule and scorn of other males. Men evaluate each other by how well they fit the ideal masculine model. Role-playing masculinity becomes a way of life, and men lose touch with their real feelings. They work hard at living up to what they're "supposed" to be.

FEELINGS

What does living up to the ideal cost? For many it's suppression of feelings from early childhood. Paul's feelings of sadness and pain were not acceptable. If he gave in to them, he became a sissy, crybaby, weakling, soft, baby, wimp. Those feelings are weak and disgraceful and unmanly.

What do men do with feelings of tenderness and love? There are few ways for males to express those feelings. It is acceptable to put your arms around a female, but not another male. In fact, tender, loving feelings toward another male may very well frighten a man into thinking he might be homosexual.

Because men don't learn to express their gentler feelings verbally, they can't tell women how they feel about them. Some men can express loving feelings only through sex. Other men have looked at sex as proof of their manhood, and no real love is expressed that way. Reaching the goal to prove to themselves that they are "real" men is their only purpose. If loving feelings surface, they can't be expressed; they have to be pushed down and suppressed again.

Boys lose out on being hugged and nurtured. Parents, especially fathers but mothers also, don't want their sons to grow up to be sissies. When little girls are hurt, fathers will hug them, dry their tears, and say, "Is my little girl hurt?" Boys hear, "Big boys don't cry." Girls can say, "I love you, Mom; I love you, Dad." Boys might tell their mother that they love her, but telling their father would be less likely.

Boys whose fathers are not bound by the sex-role stereotype may get the hugging and touching from them. Their father might say, "I love you, Son." In that case, boys may be able to say, "I love you, Dad." However, even such boys may stop saying "I love you." When boys learn that only girls play with dolls, they also learn that only girls say, "I love you." In that period when gender identity is so important, holding rigidly to the sex-role stereotypes becomes of vital importance as well. Boys soon know that showing loving feelings isn't acceptable for men.

For many males, the tender, gentle, loving side of their

personality is either not developed or underdeveloped. Those feelings are weak and feminine and unacceptable in the male sex-role stereotype. A most important part of being human is denied to those who try to live up to the stereotype.

PHYSICAL APPEARANCE

Strong, powerful, athletic, muscular describe the masculine physical ideal. Height and size indicate strength and power. Not every male is tall and muscular. Some who are short, slender, or of slight build feel less of a man. They try to make up for their size in a variety of ways. Some become aggressive and gain a reputation for being tough and willing to take on anyone. Others take risks to prove they're fearless. Working out to build a strong, muscular body is a way of feeling more manly. Body-building gives a feeling of strength and power.

As Mr. Garrett reminded Paul, sex is one of the important ways that males think they prove their manhood. Being attractive to women becomes a sign of masculinity. If you don't measure up to the physical ideal, females are as critical as males. Boys want to go with attractive girls because others judge them by the girls they attract. Girls also are judged by the boys they go with. A boy who doesn't measure up to the physical stereotype is often rejected by girls. It's very painful to feel rejection because of your physical appearance; it can rob you of your self-esteem.

The pressures from the sex-role stereotype of the strong, powerful, muscular, athletic male cause young men emotional pain that they may never mention. Paul's feeling of disappointing his father was very painful to him. He didn't mention some of the indignities he probably experienced from his peers because of his lack of athletic skills. If you're uncoordinated and not good in sports, you suffer the put-downs of those who are. What a horrible feeling to be the last one chosen for a team.

When you don't have to live up to the ideal of the athletic male, you'll be able to accept yourself as you are. Your masculinity won't be on the line. Paul was beginning to understand this about himself. He no longer wanted to live up to the stereotype. That's the first step in realizing that it has nothing to do with being a man. Not every male fits the physical stereotype because human beings come in different sizes and shapes. They also come with different interests and talents. While worrying about not meeting the stereotype, you may be neglecting the development of a special talent that you don't consider masculine enough. You could lose a special part of yourself and your humanness because of sexism.

CONSEQUENCES OF SEXISM FOR MALES

Males pay a high price for maintaining the stereotype. They become separated from their feelings and emotions very early. They role-play life. Out of touch with their feelings, they try to act the way men are supposed to act. Following the sex role becomes a way of life. As long as a male lives up to the role, he's a man. When he fails, self-doubt and feelings of worthlessness come. There's a greater need to meet the requirements of the sex role, and that demands that he give up a part of himself. He gives up the feelings that are the most human part of himself.

Women expect men to live up to the stereotype. They are contemptuous of men who don't. Women who follow the female stereotype expect men to take the leadership role in a relationship. They expect men to be all the things the stereotype says they are. They are as sexist toward men as they accuse men of being toward women.

Paul couldn't be what the sex role demanded. He didn't look at the sex role and think there might be something wrong with it. He felt there was something wrong with him. Because he couldn't live up to the sex role, Paul was paying for it with his self-esteem. In addition, he was denying an important part of himself.

Denying self is the way men can live up to the stereotype. They become shells, empty of feelings but full of the fear of failure. Paul kept wondering why he was different, why he couldn't be what he was supposed to be. He felt he was a failure in many ways, but he hadn't completely lost touch with his inner being, that feeling part of himself. Fortunately, he talked to Mr. Garrett, who understood the binds of the male sex-role stereotype. With support, Paul can release himself from the consequences of trying to live up to the sex-role ideal.

BREAKING THE BONDS OF THE STEREOTYPE

Finding release from the stereotype is not a sudden, overnight event. Changing lifetime patterns takes slow, careful, thoughtful work. It means questioning behavior, searching for options, and choosing what's best for you. That isn't something you do lightly or quickly. If you want to begin freeing yourself from sexism toward males (whether you're male or female), the following are some steps that will give you a start.

Support.   Find support for changes you want to make. That support can come from parents, a teacher, a counselor, friends, the parent of a friend, or community groups. Find others, male and female, who feel as you do. Often feminist groups are very supportive of males who want to be free of stereotypes. Cultivate friendships with males who are caring and supportive rather than competitive and defensive of their masculine image.

Labels. Become aware of how the labels of "coward," "wimp," "weakling," and other that imply a loss of manhood affect you. See if your behavior is influenced by those labels. Accepting the labels and reacting to them will keep you in the stereotype bind. If you are putting those labels on yourself or others, it's time to recognize them as poisonous and get rid of them.

Emotions. Accept yourself as being human. That means accepting your feelings of fear, affection, resentment, boredom, longing, sadness, hurt, frustration, and all others that the stereotype tells you are unacceptable. Feelings tell you what's true about you. Men have been taught that feelings are an interference or a threat that needs to be controlled. The classification of emotions as feminine has kept men from their humanness. Welcome your feelings and become a complete person.

Be Nonjudgmental. Develop an attitude of not making judgments based on the male sex-role stereotype. Pay attention to your reactions to yourself and others. Be aware when you're making judgments according to the stereotype. At those times tell yourself that being one's self is more important than living up to the stereotype. You can change within yourself. When you do, you'll find that you are more productive and your life is more fulfilling. You'll be on your way to freedom from the sex-role bind.

CHAPTER 10

Coping with Sexism

After discussing and planning for two hours, the group were winding up their meeting. Stan reached for the potato chips and said, "You know, Chris, when you suggested we do our project on sexism, I thought it was really a stupid subject. Then when I got sexism at school as my topic, I thought I'd be bored. I was really disgusted."

"Why didn't you say something?" Colleen asked.

"Well, to tell the truth, I didn't want to be the only one to object," Stan replied rather sheepishly.

"That's wild," Alex said. "I thought it was a lousy subject too."

"Not to leave out the female negative vote, I didn't like it either," Pam said. "I was with you about sexism at school, Stan."

"I wasn't too thrilled either," Ellen said. "But we all got pretty involved in it once we started."

As they ate chips and drank Cokes, the group talked about how the project had affected them. Chris spoke of how much Paul's report about the influence of sexism on males affected her. "I never thought about it that way before," Chris said.

"You made me see how much pressure is put on guys to be macho," Colleen admitted to Paul. "Girls want guys to be macho in some ways and not in others. It's like, act the way guys are supposed to act, be big and strong, but don't be sexist. It's pretty confusing. We want it all rolled up in one person of the opposite sex."

The boys agreed with Colleen. They said they were glad she could see their side of it.

"When you were making the point about songs pushing sex and victimizing females, Alex, I thought of what it does to guys too," Paul said.

"Oh, man, I never thought of that." Chris looked a little startled. "Everything that I see as victimizing females is giving males the message that they're supposed to treat females that way."

"Yeah," Stan said, "you have to do that to be a man. I never thought of it that way before."

"That's pretty heavy stuff," Gina said. "No wonder guys act the way they do."

"Not all guys act macho," Paul reminded her. That brought on a discussion of what it's like not to be macho or want to be. The girls said they understood more about the pressure put on guys, and they wanted to know how guys could resist it.

"Talking to Mr. Garrett helped me a lot," Paul confided. "He told me to look for support from people who aren't into macho. He suggested a book on assertiveness, and when I was looking for it in the library I found another one called *Coping Through Self-Esteem*. I realized that it takes self-esteem to stand up for what you believe in. That's where I'm going to start."

Paul's comment turned the discussion to what action

each group member had decided on as a result of working on the project. The girls wanted to work on a way to confront the boys who made rude, sexist remarks at school. Alex and Stan said they wouldn't participate in hassling the girls at school anymore. When Ellen asked if that meant they'd hassle girls outside of school, they laughed and agreed to cut out all sexist hassling. However, they reserved the right to be sexist when they were with guys only. That brought a challenge from Paul, who felt that saying sexist things around the guys would encourage them to continue their sexist behavior toward the girls.

The boys wanted to know what the girls planned to do about their sexist comments. Admitting they were guilty of sexist remarks about boys, the girls agreed to work on their language, too. Chris reminded the group that both males and females made sexist comments about their own sex, too. The group agreed to work on getting rid of sexist remarks about anyone.

"I need some help from you," Chris said. "How can I let Mr. Bradley know that I don't like being told I'm not qualified to be his chemistry aide because I'm a female."

Paul suggested talking to Mr. Garrett about it. Gina said she thought Ms. Foley would be helpful. Everyone had an opinion about which adults at school would be supportive. They reached the conclusion that getting help from some adult she trusted at school would be the best strategy for Chris.

"Now that school's taken care of, what about other things?" Pam wanted to know.

Alex asked Pam what she meant by other things. Pam said that she wanted to be less sexist around her younger brother and sister. She didn't want to take on her parents, but she thought she could talk about the sexism in commercials with the little kids.

"We can watch what we say, too," Colleen suggested, "so we don't add to the sexism they hear from other people. I'm going to be more nonsexist in the gifts I give my little brother. I'm thinking about giving him some string for his birthday next month and teaching him how to macramé. I'm going to encourage him to practice piano and give concerts for me. I can take a few minutes once a week to listen to him."

The group talked about ways they could influence those younger than themselves to be more flexible and to cross the sex-role barrier. Talk of crossing that barrier brought up the subject of jobs. Chris said she had half a mind to put in an application at Mr. Crawford's print shop, but she didn't want to work for such a male chauvinist. When Alex called her on sexist name-calling, Chris maintained that she was just calling him what he was. "At least I didn't say he was a chauvinist pig," she concluded with an innocent look. She put up her arms to protect herself from the pillows being thrown at her.

When the horseplay stopped, Ellen said she planned to go to the career center at school. She wanted to look at descriptions of jobs that she hadn't considered before. "I'm going to take the career counseling workshop, too," she concluded.

Gina confided that her parents had pushed her into business courses so she could get a job when she finished school. After hearing how women get stuck in low-paying office jobs, she said she had decided to talk to her counselor about how she could set her sights a little higher. Gina also accepted Ellen's invitation to join her in exploring opportunities through the career center.

"Well, I guess it's my turn," Alex said. "I've already told you some of the ways we can influence the media. I think letter-writing is something I can do."

"Do you mean you're going to write a letter now or later if you happen to get around to it?" asked Chris.

"I have something in mind right now." Alex had everyone's attention. "I'm going to write to Road Racers. You know, the cars that are advertised on the cartoon shows. They have a race track, and three boys race their cars. My little sister told me she wished she had one of those. I'm going to write the company and tell them they should have girls in the commercials too. I'm going to suggest to my parents that they get her a Road Racer for Christmas."

"All right, Alex!" cheered Colleen. "What about you, Stan?"

"I've been thinking about what you said, Paul," Stan began. "You know, about hanging around when the talk gets rank about girls. Sometimes I don't like it—especially when it's about a girl I like. I never say anything, though. I'm still not going to say anything, but I won't hang around when the talk gets rough. I guess that's a first step toward doing something."

The group agreed that it was a step in the right direction. Gina looked thoughtful for a minute and said, "I've been thinking about what you said the other day, Chris, that anything we do will affect other people and have a ripple effect. I was thinking that looking into a different career really isn't much. But the ripple effect was already working there because it was Ellen who made me think of it. We don't know whom we'll influence. Some of the other guys may see you walk away, Stan, and decide to go with you. They may just be waiting for someone else to leave first. Who knows?"

After talking about the possibilities of influencing others, the group broke up. They left with a feeling of satisfaction that Paul summed up for the group: "No matter what grade I get on this, I'm glad I worked on the project."

* * *

Sexism is a part of your world. It will continue to be in your world. Though it's unlikely that sexism will be eliminated, its growth can be slowed. Perhaps in time its growth will be stopped. When it stops growing, the chances of its death will increase. Though you probably won't see the end of sexism, you can contribute to its end. Getting rid of sexism doesn't mean making the sexes the same. It means allowing everyone to enjoy unlimited choices for living life to the fullest.

The place to start eliminating sexism is in yourself. You're now aware of what sexism is. You're also aware of your own sexist views and behaviors. You can make changes in your behavior. Start with something small that you know you can do. You can't change all your sexist behavior overnight. You didn't accumulate your attitudes and behavior in a day. However, awareness of your own sexism and working on one behavior change will lead to other changes.

As you change, you will influence those around you. You can have a ripple effect. You can work on your own sexism and influence others to become aware of theirs. When you become a parent, you can raise your children without the restrictions of sex-role stereotypes. The ideas for coping with sexism in this book are just a starting point for you. Free yourself of your restricting sexism. Give yourself the gift of choices you thought you didn't have. Treat yourself to the joy of unlimited options. See yourself as a human being first and as a male or female second. Allow yourself to explore avenues once closed to you because of your sexist thinking. Reach for wholeness as a human being. The decision is yours.

Further Reading

Backhouse, Constance, and Cohen, Leah. *Sexual Harassment on the Job*. Englewood Cliffs, NJ: Prentice-Hall, 1981.

Berger, Gilda. *Women, Wages, and Work*. New York: Franklin Watts, 1986.

Black, Beryl. *Coping with Sexual Harassment*. New York: Rosen Publishing Group, 1987.

Frazier, N., and Sadker, M. *Sexism in School and Society*. New York: Harper and Row, 1973.

Gersoni-Stavn, Diane. *Sexism and Youth*. New York: R.R. Bowker Co., 1974.

Goldberg, Herb. *The Hazards of Being Male*. New York: Signet Books, 1976.

————. *The New Male*. New York: Signet Books, 1979.

Maccoby, E.E., and Jacklin, C.N. *The Psychology of Sex Differences*. Stanford, CA: Stanford University Press, 1974.

McFarland, Rhoda. *Coping Through Assertiveness*. New York: Rosen Publishing Group, 1986.

————. *Coping Through Self-Esteem*. New York: Rosen Publishing Group, 1988.

Ms. Foundation, Inc. *Free to Be . . . You and Me*. New York: Bantam Books, 1987.

Pogrebin, Letty Cottin. *Growing Up Free—Raising Your Child in the 80's*. New York: McGraw-Hill, 1980.

Stein, Sara Bonnett. *Girls and Boys*. New York: Scribner's, 1983

Zilbergeld, Bernie, Ph.D. *Male Sexuality*. New York: Bantam Books, 1978.

Index